Greek Literature in the Roman Empire

Classical World Series

Aristophanes and his Theatre of the Absurd, Paul Cartledge
Art and the Romans, Anne Haward
Athens and Sparta, S. Todd
Athens under the Tyrants, J. Smith
Athletics in the Ancient World, Zahra Newby
Attic Orators, Michael Edwards
Augustan Rome, Andrew Wallace-Hadrill
Cicero and the End of the Roman Republic, Thomas Wiedemann
Classical Archaeology in the Field, S.J. Hill, L. Bowkett and
   K. & D. Wardle
Classical Epic: Homer and Virgil, Richard Jenkyns
Democracy in Classical Athens, Christopher Carey
Environment and the Classical World, Patricia Jeskins
Greece and the Persians, John Sharwood Smith
Greek and Roman Historians, Timothy E. Duff
Greek and Roman Medicine, Helen King
Greek Architecture, R. Tomlinson
Greek Literature in the Roman Empire, Jason König
Greek Tragedy: An Introduction, Marion Baldock
Greek Vases, Elizabeth Moignard
Julio-Claudian Emperors, T. Wiedemann
Lucretius and the Didactic Epic, Monica Gale
Morals and Values in Ancient Greece, John Ferguson
Mycenaean World, K. & D. Wardle
Plato's Republic and the Greek Enlightenment, Hugh Lawson-Tancred
Plays of Euripides, James Morwood
Plays of Sophocles, A.F. Garvie
Political Life in the City of Rome, J.R. Patterson
Religion and the Greeks, Robert Garland
Religion and the Romans, Ken Dowden
Roman Architecture, Martin Thorpe
Roman Britain, S.J. Hill and S. Ireland
Roman Frontiers in Britain, David Breeze
Roman Satirists and Their Masks, Susanna Braund
Slavery in Classical Greece, N. Fisher
Women in Classical Athens, Sue Blundell

Classical World Series

GREEK LITERATURE IN THE ROMAN EMPIRE

Jason König

B L O O M S B U R Y
LONDON • NEW DELHI • NEW YORK • SYDNEY

Bloomsbury Academic
An imprint of Bloomsbury Publishing Plc

50 Bedford Square
London
WC1B 3DP
UK

1385 Broadway
New York
NY 10018
USA

www.bloomsbury.com

Bloomsbury is a registered trade mark of Bloomsbury Publishing Plc

First published in 2009 by Bristol Classical Press an imprint of
Gerald Duckworth & Co. Ltd.

British Library Cataloguing-in-Publication Data
A catalogue record for this book is available from the British Library.

ISBN: PB: 978-1-8539-9713-6
ePUB: 978-1-4725-2132-3
ePDF: 978-1-4725-2131-6

Library of Congress Cataloging-in-Publication Data
A catalog record for this book is available from the Library of Congress.

Contents

Preface 6
Map 7
Introduction 7

1. Novels 11
2. Satire 27
3. Oratory 41
4. Philosophy 54
5. Science and Miscellanism 66
6. History and Geography 77
7. Biography 86
8. Conclusion: Poetry and Prose 99

Suggestions for Further Reading 105
Questions for Further Study and Discussion 111
Timeline 114
Index 117

Preface

I am very grateful to those who have read sections of this book in draft and discussed with me the example passages I have chosen. In particular, I am grateful to students in my St Andrews honours courses on 'Greek Literature in the Roman Empire' and 'The Ancient and Modern Novel' over the last five years, who have helped me to get to grips in more depth with many of these texts. I would like to thank the anonymous readers for the Press, who have made many helpful suggestions. Last but not least, I am grateful also to the many friends and colleagues whose publications in this field have helped me to further my own understanding of the many works I discuss: for reasons of space it has been possible, in the suggestions on further reading at the end of the book, to list only a small number of those works.

Note on periodisation: the main focus of this book is the period 31 BCE to 235 CE, but I also regularly look back to the literature of classical and Hellenistic Greece and of the late Roman Republic. I also look ahead to the later third century, and even occasionally into the fourth century after the emperor Constantine's Christianisation of the empire. I have followed standard periodisations for Greek history and literature: archaic (roughly 800-479 BCE); classical (479-323 BCE); Hellenistic (323-31 BCE); Imperial (31 BCE to roughly 300 CE). I also occasionally use the word 'Republican' to describe the period of Roman history up to 31 BCE.

There is no consensus about the most desirable spelling of Greek names and book titles. I have generally preferred to stick closely to the original Greek form in transliterating, except where a Latinate spelling is so familiar that it would look peculiar in its Greek form

I have used the word 'Hellenic' interchangeably for 'Greek'.

My aim throughout the book has been to balance an accessible and comprehensive overview with close attention to particular passages, in the hope of conveying some of the fascinations and challenges of the reading experience imperial Greek literature offers. All the translations are my own.

St Andrews
January 2009

Introduction

The Greek cities of the eastern Mediterranean world began to have sustained contact with Rome in the second half of the third century BCE. Roman domination over the area was established and consolidated during the next two centuries or so only through a gradual process, relying on diplomacy and the threat of force as much as actual military conquest. Throughout that time Greek cities under Roman rule were left for the most part with a strong degree of political and cultural autonomy. In the more settled conditions of the Roman Imperial period (from 31 BCE onwards, the year when Augustus, Rome's first emperor, defeated his rival for power, Mark Antony), that tradition of Greek autonomy led to an increasing flourishing of Greek city life, which reached its height in the second and early third centuries CE, the period on which this book is mainly focused. A very large proportion of the territory of the Roman Empire covered traditionally Greek-speaking areas, not only the traditional centres of mainland Greece, but also the wealthy cities in Asia Minor (now western Turkey), not to mention a whole string of others dotted around the eastern Mediterranean, from the Greek-speaking cities of Southern

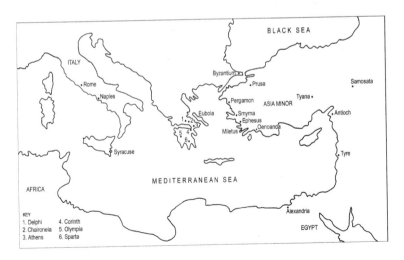

Italy, to the great cultural centre of Alexandria on the north coast of Egypt. The Greek cities of the east eagerly celebrated their Greek identity and local traditions, for example through enormous numbers of new public buildings and festivals, paid for by wealthy inhabitants in exchange for honours from their home cities. Greek was the *lingua franca* of the Roman Empire. Even Rome itself was home to a significant Greek-speaking population. Increasingly large numbers of Greeks served in the Roman senate as the second century went on, some of them even holding the supreme office of consul.

All of that coincided with a flourishing of Greek culture. One of the most conspicuous signs of this flourishing was the growth of Greek rhetoric. Orators known as 'sophists' (named after the sophists – itinerant intellectuals – of classical Greece) not only taught rhetoric, but also toured the empire giving speeches on subjects taken from (among other things) classical Greek history, and showing off their command of the traditional 'Attic' dialect of classical Athens. Many of these figures won enormous wealth and political influence through their rhetorical prowess. The literary activity of the period has sometimes been named as the 'Second Sophistic' (a term used twice by the third-century CE author Philostratus) in an acknowledgement of the importance of these orators (although focusing on sophistic rhetoric at the expense of other genres can lead one to underestimate vastly the richness and variety of the Greek literature of the Roman Empire, and the term 'Second Sophistic' is now much less widely used than it used to be). Knowledge of Greek literary culture could be enormously prestigious even for members of the Roman elite, although their engagement with Greek culture was often selective. The volume of Greek literature from this period is enormous, especially if one includes the early Christian writing composed in Greek from the mid-first century onwards, literature which was from the beginning closely bound up with Greco-Roman models. I include brief discussion of that Christian literature from time to time in the chapters which follow.

The Greek literature of this period is not just abundant; it also contains, I want to suggest, some of the most fascinating and challenging of all surviving classical literature. That claim would have seemed like an odd one to make even just a few decades ago. Late nineteenth-century scholarship – inspired by idealised notions of classical Athens as the high-point of ancient Greek culture – came to view later Greek literature as degenerate, a symptom of the decline of the Greek spirit into nostalgia and subservience. Certainly it is hard to deny that it is a body of literature obsessed with the past. However, there has been increasing appreciation and analysis of Imperial Greek literature in recent decades, perhaps in part because of an increasing tendency within our own contemporary culture to view lateness, derivativeness, marginality and hybrid identity as things to be celebrated rather than condemned. That change of attitude in many ways takes us closer to earlier centuries of modern European culture: Lucian, Heliodorus, Plutarch and others have all at various times, in the Renaissance and after, been among the most read and most influential of all classical authors.

This volume offers a broad introduction to Imperial Greek literature, not only for those who are studying these texts at school or undergraduate level, but also for others who are coming to this body of material for the first time. I aim to set some of the more familiar texts – for example, Lucian and the Greek novels, discussed in Chapters 1 and 2 respectively – against their wider cultural and literary background, while also opening up for study, in later chapters, some of the more difficult material which is less frequently studied. Some areas of Greek Imperial culture – not least the obsession with sophistic rhetoric mentioned briefly above – are at first sight quite alien to modern literary experience (despite the claims I have just made about changing tastes). My aim is to bring to life some of the thrill and fascination they held, at their best, for their original audiences. The book is structured on a genre-by-genre basis. However, one of its recurring themes will be the difficulty of maintaining boundaries of that sort: one of the hallmarks of the writing of this period is its great generic inventiveness which combines different traditions freely in the quest for new ways of writing. Another of the book's aims is to draw out the way in which this literature speaks to the concerns of its contemporary audiences, even when it appears at first sight to be quite detached from the real world. Literary practice mattered for its audiences and practitioners. That is partly because literary learning was itself so prestigious – an essential marker of high social status. More importantly, many of these texts used fantastical narratives or accounts of the Greek past to address issues of contemporary concern, as we shall see straight away in Chapter 1 for the Greek novels. That said, one should perhaps not be too obsessed with the task of setting these texts into a wider political and cultural context if that stops one from seeing the pleasures they have to offer. The best reason of all for reading the Greek literature of the Roman Empire, as I hope to show, is to enjoy it, as its original readers and audiences must often have done, appreciating its virtuoso displays of ingenuity, fantasy and erudition.

Chapter 1

Novels

Introducing Heliodorus

There are five fully surviving texts which between them are usually labelled as 'the Greek novels'. As we shall see, focusing narrowly on these five texts can lead one to underestimate the richness of the period's prose fiction tradition. Nevertheless for the first part of this chapter they form my main point of discussion. For reasons of space I concentrate in particular on one text, Heliodorus' *Ethiopian Tale.*

Imagine, for a moment, a beach at sunrise: on it, a morass of dead bodies, some of them still twitching, and strewn between them the remains of a meal, wine and blood mingling in the sand. On a rock in the middle of the carnage sits a divinely beautiful girl holding a bow and quiver on one arm, and in the other arm cradling the head of a wounded youth covered with blood. That is the scene – almost cinematic in its impact – which greets us at the beginning of Heliodorus' novel. We see it through the eyes of barbarians, Egyptian bandits who have come down to the shore in the hope of plunder but are now stopped short by what they see. We share their bewilderment; we, like them, are challenged to decipher the identity of the girl and the events which have led to this slaughter. That theme of decipherment runs right through the ten books (more than 200 pages in English translation) which follow: not until the end of Book 5 do we finally discover the cause of these deaths on the beach; and not until Book 10 do we uncover all the secrets of the girl's story. The structure is wonderfully complex, full of flashbacks and stories within stories, and characters who are not what they seem, rivalling the most ingenious literary game-playing of postmodern fiction.

At the centre of the story are Charikleia and her fiancé Theagenes, the two figures on the beach. They meet in Delphi, one of the great religious centres of the Greek world; they run away together, in the company of the Egyptian wise-man Kalasiris who has helped to bring them together. A number of times they are separated, facing threats to their safety and their chastity from pirates and lustful rulers; all the time they are swept further and further southwards through Egypt, away from the Mediterranean. In

Book 10, finally, they are carried as prisoners of war to the Ethiopian capital Meroe to be sacrificed publicly as a thanks offering for the Ethiopian king's victory. And here, suddenly, in the final pages, it is revealed (although we, the readers, along with Charikleia, have already had the truth made clear to us in Book 4) that the white Charikleia is herself the daughter of the black Ethiopian king and queen: the queen, we are told, had been looking at a picture of the Greek heroine Andromeda at the moment when Charikleia was conceived; the baby, born white for that reason, was abandoned at birth together with a series of recognition tokens which she still carries with her, and which now allow her identity to be established. The closing moments of the novel anticipate the impending marriage of the hero and heroine.

Ancient and modern fiction

How does Heliodorus' novel look by modern standards? The novel genre is still often regarded as a modern invention. For example, Cervantes' *Don Quixote*, published in two volumes in 1605 and 1615, with its parody of chivalric romance, is often viewed as an important step towards the modern novel, unlike anything which had come before. Similarly, it is commonplace to see the 'realism' of eighteenth-century English fiction – influenced by the development of new capitalist and protestant ideas about the individual within society – as something which separates the novels of that period from the 'romance' traditions which preceded them. Clearly both of those claims do have some validity. However, the popularity and continuing influence of the ancient novels across these centuries should make us very wary of accepting those interpretations wholesale: the split between ancient romance and modern fiction is, on closer inspection, not quite so clear-cut. The ancient novels were widely translated into modern European languages between the sixteenth and eighteenth centuries, and had an enormous influence on the formation of modern European novel traditions and indeed on many of the new kinds of novel-writing just mentioned. Heliodorus in particular was widely admired and imitated. Cervantes himself paid tribute to the *Ethiopian Tale* by imitating it in his work *Persiles and Sigismunda* (a labyrinthine story of hero and heroine travelling through strange lands in the frozen north, published in 1617, the year after his death) which he clearly viewed as the crowning ambition of his career: 'a book which dares to compete with Heliodorus' as he put it in advertising the work before its publication in the prologue to his *Novelas Ejemplares*. The *Persiles* achieved wide and instant success to match that of *Don Quixote* (which seems, by contrast, to have been composed more casually, and never intended as such a prestigious literary undertaking).

However, despite its importance for the formation of modern novel traditions, Heliodorus' work (like that of his ancient novelistic counterparts, and indeed like Cervantes' *Persiles*) has not always appealed to modern taste in more recent centuries. By the standards of modern fiction there is relatively little concern with intricate characterisation of the kind which seems to take us inside a character's mind, little sign of the complex shades of perception and motivation which mark so much of the great novel writing of the eighteenth and nineteenth centuries and which still influence modern taste. Emotion, as so often in other ancient literature, tends to be described in quite stylised terms. We should perhaps acknowledge that fictional ways of describing feelings and characters are stylised and dependent on convention in all ages: no doubt the idioms of modern fiction will seem artificial to future ages, even if they do not now seem to to us. There are also plenty of exceptions to the stereotype of the ancient novels as texts which lack any attention to in-depth characterisation. The scene in Chariton's novel *Chaireas and Kallirhoe* where the heroine Kallirhoe debates whether to remarry for the sake of her unborn child (2.11) is often cited as an example of enormous pathos. Nevertheless it is clear that many of the pleasures of these texts lie elsewhere, founded on ingenious plotting, virtuoso set-piece description, and inventive reworking of earlier genres into innovative new forms. Some of those qualities can be explained by the role of rhetoric within ancient society and ancient literary culture – something which is quite alien to most present-day fiction. The exercise of constructing ingenious speeches and descriptions appropriate to imaginary scenarios was a standard part of ancient rhetorical education and clearly influenced the Greek novelists heavily.

Pleasures and challenges

It would be wrong, however, to imagine that these novels were read simply as examples of detached literary play. For most of us, one reason for reading stories (or watching them on screen) is that they give us images against which to measure up our own lives, even if that process often happens at an unconscious level, without being phrased in such solemn terms. I want to suggest in what follows that much the same is true of the Greek novels of the Roman Empire. They give their original readers a way of imagining – albeit in exaggerated and unrealistic terms – the hold of fate over the lives of individuals. They present pictures of foreign lands and barbarian culture which raise questions – as Greek writing about foreign peoples always had done, as far back as Herodotus or even the *Odyssey* – about what being Greek really means. In addition, they offer fantasies of elite identity against which their readers can measure themselves, through the impossibly beautiful hero and heroine who lie at the centre of all of them. Many of the heroines in particular are appealingly independent-minded and self-reliant. All five of these texts end with the reunion of hero and heroine. The pleasure offered to us in these moments of resolution is familiar to us from modern films and novels, whose obsession with 'closure' – happy resolution and tying up of loose ends – is inherited in part from classical models of narrative. At the same time these texts often take quite a playful attitude to the idealised characters they present to us, questioning the degree to which they can separate them from the absurd and grotesque elements of the world they find around them.

Heliodorus' work has obvious affinities with the four other surviving 'Greek novels': Xenophon of Ephesus' *Ephesian Tale*, Chariton's *Chaireas and Kallirhoe*, Longus' *Daphnis and Chloe* and Achilles Tatius' *Leukippe and Kleitophon*. The dating of these works is much disputed, but it seems likely that most if not all of them were composed between the first and third centuries CE (although some scholars place Chariton's work rather earlier than that; and Heliodorus' *Ethiopian Tale* is sometimes dated as late as the late fourth century). Each of these texts follows the same basic plot pattern of lovers separated and endangered before finally being reunited. Each of them also stamps that basic pattern with its own distinctive approach.

Xenophon of Ephesus looks – anyway at first sight – like the least sophisticated author of the five. His work seems to be influenced at least in part by oral traditions of story-telling, using short sentences and simple vocabulary and with many repetitions of phrasing and plot patterns. Despite that simplicity, however, the *Ephesian Tale* offers many pleasures – not least in its nightmarishly claustrophobic vision of individuals at the mercy of fate, which is mirrored by the claustrophobic repetitiveness of the text's language. Xenophon's heroine and hero, Antheia and Habrokomes, are repeatedly captured and threatened with rape and execution – held by pirates, bandits, Roman provincial governors and brothelkeepers – before their final reunion.

Chariton, by contrast with Xenophon, sets his work in the classical past. He takes his protagonists further afield. Kallirhoe is the beautiful daughter of the famous Sicilian general Hermokrates who fought against the Athenian invasion in the late fifth-century BCE. She and her husband Chaireas are wrenched by fate away from the safe haven of their home, and find themselves in the second half of the novel in Persia. There Kallirhoe's Greek beauty outshines the beauty of all the women of Persia and attracts the attentions of the Persian king. Chaireas, meanwhile, finds himself leading the forces of the Egyptians in a series of military victories against Persia, and is finally reunited with Kallirhoe only when she is delivered to him as a prisoner of war. The novel ends with their triumphal return to Syracuse.

Longus takes a quite different approach to geographical space: his is the only one of the five novels to be set in the same place throughout. It tells the story of two children from separate families, Daphnis and Chloe, abandoned by their parents in the countryside and brought up by two separate sets of rustic foster-parents. Their growing love for each other is matched by the changing rhythms of the seasons. We also see them fending off a string of increasingly violent intruders who attempt to capture or seduce them, before finally their true parents are revealed – wealthy inhabitants of the city – clearing the way for their marriage. The text plays with the question of whether love can ever be natural and untaught. We see them struggling to understand what love is and how it works. One scene, for example, shows Daphnis attempting unsuccessfully to have sex with Chloe by copying the goats they have seen mating in the fields: '… lying down with her he lay there for a long time, and then, not knowing how to do any of the things for which he was swelling with lust, he stood her up again and embraced her from behind, imitating the goats'. Daphnis, we hear, 'felt even more confused than before and sat down and wept at the thought that he was more uneducated than the rams at the deeds of love' (3.14). In an ingenious 'pastoralisation' of the conventions of the novel, their loss of virginity is delayed in this scene and others like it, not, as for the heroes and heroines of the other texts, because of their desire for chastity, but instead because of their rustic ignorance.

Achilles Tatius' text, finally, is the only one of these five works to use a first-person narrator. His is also the most obviously salacious of the novels, tempting us to share the narrator's voyeuristic perspective – not least in a number of false execution scenes, including one where the narrator Kleitophon's fiancée Leukippe appears to have been disembowelled by a group of bandits who then feast on her entrails (a trick, as it turns out) (3.15). Nevertheless even this text is careful to wrap its more risqué elements, albeit playfully, in the cloak of respectability. At one point, for example, shortly before his reunion with Leukippe, the hero allows himself to be seduced by an older woman, Melite, and then gives us a sophistical speech of justification for his actions, claiming that he acted through pity for Melite, because she was so hopelessly in love with him, and so cannot be counted as unfaithful (5.27).

Readership

The question of who might have read these texts is a difficult one. Some scholars have argued that the genre was intended to have a populist appeal, perhaps particularly for female readers, given the relatively high number of very assertive female characters they contain. Others have stressed the complexity with which the novels weave together allusions to earlier literature and have taken that as a sign that they are aimed at highly educated, erudite readers. Neither of those solutions is satisfactory when stated in such over-simplified terms. For one thing, we might expect a different picture for different texts. Xenophon of Ephesus, for example, even if we accept that it is not an unsophisticated narrative, has very little of the complex play with earlier literature just mentioned. It seems likely, too, that many of these texts aim to appeal at a number different levels at the same time.

Most importantly, perhaps, we need to acknowledge that these are texts which repeatedly prompt us as readers to reflect upon our own relationship with what we are reading. Far from appealing straightforwardly to one particular audience, in other words, these are texts which raise challenging and playful questions about how the act of reading affects our view of our own identity. Heliodorus, for example, fills his novel with scenes of characters listening to stories (and indeed looking at pictures) and reacting in a wide spectrum of different ways, ranging from naïve and gullible listeners to sophisticated interpreters who go at least some way towards understanding the divine hand which guides Theagenes and Charikleia on their way via the author's pen. The perplexed barbarians whose perspective we share in the opening scene are at the less sophisticated end of that spectrum, as is the crowd of Ethiopian onlookers who watch the denouement in the final scenes in Book 10, and who must guess at what is happening because they cannot understand the Greek which is being spoken by the main characters. Do we share their bewilderment and their interpretative naivety, the text seems to ask us, or can we decipher what is in front of us any better?

Longus, rather differently, tempts us to sympathise with the innocent perspective of his protagonists while also at the same time confronting us with our own educated, urban perspective. Daphnis, for example, describes the physical symptoms of his infatuation in the only language he knows, the language of the countryside, without ever having heard of love:

'That was the first time he admired her hair, for its golden colour, and her face, because it was truly whiter even than the milk of goats; it was if that was the first time he had acquired eyes, as if he had been blind before ... his flock was neglected, his pipes were thrown aside, and his face was paler than summer grass' (1.17). In reading that passage, can we fail to see (if we are educated Greek readers) that Daphnis is unwittingly replicating the symptoms of love described in Sappho's famous poem on the bodily effects of desire? (Sappho 31, following the numbering of Lobel and Page, *Poetarum Lesbiorum Fragmenta*). When Chloe rescues Daphnis from a wolf trap by innocently unwinding her breast band in order to use it as a rope to pull him up (1.12), can we fail to view that scene with the overtones of eroticised undressing in mind? In both cases Longus confronts us with the fact that we cannot share the innocent style of looking at the world which Daphnis and Chloe themselves display.

Literary ancestry

What, then, are the main literary influences on the Greek novels? Rhetoric I have mentioned already – but that is only one of many strands. Tragedy, epic (the *Odyssey* in particular) and comedy (especially the so-called New Comedy of the late fourth and early third century BCE) are also constant presences within these texts. The love poetry of Greek lyric leaves its mark on the works' portrayals of erotic passion. Many of them also imitate the work of Greek historians. For example, Chariton's choice of the historical character Hermokrates for his heroine's father is one of many elements which give the impression that he is deliberately rewriting the monumental, historical narrative of Thucydides from a more mundane, individual-centred perspective. Longus undertakes the most daring experiment of all in his reshaping of pastoral themes within the framework of prose fiction. Some of these texts draw also on the language of Platonic philosophical dialogue, hinting at underlying allegorical significance in these stories, while also tripping us up if we search for it too solemnly. Part of the thrill of reading the ancient novel – at least in the more allusive texts – is this the thrill of recognising quotations from earlier literature and seeing them transformed in their new context. For many critics, in fact, the novel, both ancient and modern, is defined by its capacity to incorporate many different kinds of voices and traditions. On that argument there is relatively little point in speculating about the relative influence of different genres: more important is to be alert to the effects these texts achieve by weaving together many different registers and different voices. Often that combination of apparently incompatible material has a defamiliarising effect, prompting us to look afresh at the source text, while also offering us new ways of imagining the world, giving us the opportunity to view ordinary events through a mythical or classical template. Heliodorus' opening scene of Charikleia resting on the beach with the bow on her shoulder replays the Odyssean scene of the slaughter of the suitors in the middle of their feasting: it does so in a way which makes that original scene into something new, while also enriching the world of the novel, inviting us to measure up Charikleia against the heroic figure of Odysseus just as we may measure up ourselves against her and against Theagenes.

Women in the Greek novels

I want to spend most of the rest of this chapter looking at some of the fantasy images of the *Ethiopian Tale* in more depth, with some sideways glances at the other novels along the way. Let us return first to the point I made above about the idealisation of female independence in these texts. The Odyssean characteristics given to Charikleia in that opening scene extend to much of the rest of the text. She is repeatedly shown to be more enterprising than her lover Theagenes, especially through her command of typically Odyssean skills of deception and disguise. In 1.21-3, for example, in response to the bandit chief Thyamis who wants to marry her, she wins time by an Odysseus-style lying story. She and Theagenes, she claims, are brother and sister, priestess of Artemis and priest of Apollo. They were sailing on a sacred embassy when they were ship-wrecked and driven to shore, where the sailors turned against them and tried to rob them of the vast wealth they were carrying. They resisted them by force, hence the vast slaughter on the beach (here potentially Charikleia deceives us as readers as much as Thyamis – we ourselves do not yet know the truth about the beach). She asks Thyamis for time to go to a temple of Apollo to lay aside her badge of priestly office before marrying him. Here, then, she demonstrates an Odyssean style of ingenuity. She is also similar to Odysseus in her flirtation with infidelity, although Odysseus takes that further, sleeping with both Circe and Calypso, and concealing that fact when it suits him to do so, not least in front of his wife Penelope on his return home. Theagenes' complaining response points up the risqué character of her claims: 'I understood that the story about Ionia and about losing our way to Delos was a cover for the truth, to make the listeners get lost themselves. But the business of agreeing to the marriage so readily, coming to terms with him so unequivocally, and even fixing the date, that I was neither able nor willing to accept' (1.25-6). As so often

Theagenes looks comically flat-footed and literal-minded next to his more enterprising fiancée.

However, it would be wrong to overstate the claim that the Greek novels straightforwardly uphold a model of female emancipation. In some ways, in fact, they do the opposite. It is striking, for one thing, that the heroines' independence lasts only while they are in danger and away from home. In all five of these texts we see them being swallowed up back into conventional, patriarchal models of female virtue in the final marriage and reunion scenes. That development is most striking, and disturbing, in Longus' *Daphnis and Chloe*. At the beginning of that text Chloe is free to grow up without the constraints of urban convention, but as the work goes on she becomes increasingly squeezed into a subordinate position because of her female sex, and increasingly at risk from violence at the hands of predatory males. The final marriage scenes of the novel are represented as a release from danger, as Daphnis and Chloe celebrate the new pleasures and empowerments of their rediscovered wealth and nobility, but it is also hard to avoid the feeling that these scenes at the same time represent a culmination of that pattern of increasing suppression and constraint in Chloe's transition to adulthood.

Elitist fiction?

We might even view these as very conservative texts interested ultimately in celebrating a conventional picture of idealised elite virtue directed to respectable ends within the context of the Greek city and within the institution of marriage. Some have even gone so far as to see the novels as heavily ideological fantasies, designed to bolster the confidence of the wealthy elites of the Greek-speaking Mediterranean, who set so much store by their position as inheritors of classical Greek culture in this period. That may go some way towards explaining the novelists' tendency to set their stories in the distant past rather than the Roman present (preoccupation with classical history and lack of interest in Roman-period events is a common feature of much of the literature of this period, as we shall see for Pausanias in Chapter 6). The portrayal of elite beauty also contributes to this idealising effect: we see impossibly beautiful heroes and heroines who manage to maintain their beauty, their chastity and their elite individuality even in the most threatening situations, coming away from torture and trauma magically unscarred. The link between beauty and virtue acts as an authorising fantasy of elite superiority. Low-status characters, by contrast, tend to get a bad deal: in one particularly horrifying example, not long after the fake-disembowelling scene already mentioned, Achilles Tatius' hero Kleitophon thinks he has seen his fiancée decapitated (5.7); the novel later recalls only rejoicing and relief when it turns out that a prostitute has been substituted for her at the last minute.

Nevertheless I think it would be wrong to assume that these texts are entirely serious about these fantasy images of elite superiority. In fact they constantly poke fun at them. For an example of a playful take on these themes we might turn to a later passage in Heliodorus Book 7 where Theagenes and Charikleia are reunited with each other after a considerable time apart. Charikleia has been travelling disguised as a beggar, in much the same way as Odysseus on his return home to Ithaka. She reaches the city of Memphis, in Egypt, only to see Theagenes running round the walls of the city watching the combat between Thyamis and his brother Petosiris. Their father Kalasiris, who has been travelling with Charikleia in disguise, stops their fight by revealing his identity to them (the coincidence-filled plotting, which makes Charikleia's mentor Kalasiris the father of the bandit chief from Book 1 is typical of labyrinthine, interwoven shape of the novel as a whole). At this point Charikleia, who has also joined in the chase around the walls, reveals herself to Theagenes, having spotted him from a distance:

> For the sight is often sharp in its recognition of those one loves, and often just a movement or a shape, even if it is far away, is enough to bring an image resembling the beloved before one's mind. Charikleia approached him, as if goaded into madness by the sight, and draping herself around his neck tightly she hung on to him and clung to him and greeted him with mournful cries. But Theagenes, as you would expect, on seeing her face, which had grown dirty and ugly, and her worn-out and tattered clothes, tried to push her away and elbow her aside as if she really was a beggar and a tramp. And then finally, when she refused to let go of him, since she was annoying him and blocking his view of what was happening to Kalasiris, he slapped her (7.7).

They are, predictably enough, reconciled with each other as soon as Charikleia convinces him it is her, but the comical overtones here are hard to miss. Theagenes does indeed insist on his own elite status by pushing away the low-status intruder, almost as if he is afraid of contamination by her beggarly appearance. But in doing so he throws doubt on precisely the principles of recognisability which are stated at the beginning of the passage. The fantasy of Charikleia's unparalleled beauty begins to look a little hollow at this point. And Charikleia's Odyssean moment of self-revelation, throwing off her disguise as a beggar, as the great hero does in order to strike terror into the suitors, falls decidedly flat. Similar scenes of comical non-recognition haunt some of the other novels too. The very fact that Kleitophon mistakes the headless body of an unnamed prostitute for his beloved suggests that her beauty may not be so much engraved in his heart as he claims (although the problem is of course consistent with the claim that they have had a chaste relationship since their elopement – Kleitophon may not have seen very much of her body apart from its head during that time). Later, still thinking that Leukippe is dead, Kleitophon walks straight past her without recognising her (5.17) – she has been sold as a slave and her head shaved. In these scenes, Achilles Tatius goes further than Heliodorus in contaminating the image of ideal female beauty, overlaying it with grotesque and low-status associations.

Greek identity in the novels

It is not only elite identity which the novels fantasise about and joke about, but also Greek identity. Even the brief summaries given above should make it clear that many of these texts, and particularly those of Chariton and Heliodorus, use traditions of Greek writing about foreign lands in order to celebrate the superiority of Greek culture and Greek virtues. Chaireas, in Chariton's novel, goes from powerless individual hundreds of miles from home to opponent of the military might of Persia in a matter of days. In much the same way, Kallirhoe's beauty effortlessly trumps the attractions of all the women of Persia. Similarly in Book 10 of the *Ethiopian Tale* we see Theagenes finally showing what he is made of, capturing an escaped bull single-handed, and then winning a wrestling match against a giant Ethiopian whom no one else will fight against, using traditionally Greek athletic skills. Heliodorus tells us that Theagenes is 'a man of the gymnasium, and a practitioner of athletics from his youth, fully versed in the competitive skills of Hermes [i.e. the god of the gymnasium]' (10.31). And yet of course it is clear that Heliodorus' text also complicates any straightforward assertions about Greek superiority through its revelation of the heroine's Ethiopian origins: her outstanding Greek beauty and virtue turn out not to be genetically Greek after all. Moreover, the Ethiopian king, Hydaspes, despite his endorsement of human sacrifice, is in some ways representative of ideal Greek models of kingship, dependent on the advice of the country's wise men, the 'gymnosophists' ('naked sages'). Their wisdom is represented, in other Greek writings from this period, as having much in common with the wisdom of Greek philosophy. Their civilising influence becomes clear when human sacrifice is banned from Ethiopia, on their advice, in the closing pages of Heliodorus' novel.

The basic 'return-home' plot of the *Odyssey* is reshaped in Heliodorus' version. Strictly speaking this is a return-home for Charikleia, but in terms of our own reading experience (and also for Theagenes), it is a one-way plot pattern from Greece to Ethiopia, with no return in view: it looks in the final line as though Theagenes and Charikleia are preparing to settle down to married life in Meroe. That twisting of the shape of the *Odyssey* articulates the text's ambivalence towards Greek culture. It deprives us of the Greek-centred closure of a plot like Chariton's, where Chaireas and Kallirhoe return in triumph to their Greek home in Syracuse, portraying Ethiopia instead as the symbolic centre and end-point for the work.

Not only that, but Heliodorus enacts a very double-edged picture of his own authorial identity in the extraordinary final lines of the work, where he reveals that the *Ethiopian Tale* is itself 'written by a Phoenician man from Emesa, from the family of those descended from the Sun, son of Theodosios, Heliodorus' (10.41). The text itself thus masquerades as a Greek narrative, but is unmasked, rather like Charikleia's identity, in the final lines of the text. This cunning moment of closing authorial self-revelation invites us to reassess the whole of what has gone before, and to wonder about the possibility that the novel has a more subversive and complex relation with Greek virtue and Greek narrative tradition than we might initially have assumed. Some scholars have even argued, taking their key from this passage and others like it, that the ancient novel as a genre was influenced by non-Greek story-telling traditions, as well as by the learned, sophistic currents of mainstream Greek culture.

Apuleius, Petronius, Photius and the fragments

Just as the identities of hero and heroine are not so pristine as we might at first assume, so the category of 'the Greek novel' is not nearly as clear-cut as my choice of texts so far has implied. Many critics have in the past drawn strong lines between these five Greek texts and the two fully surviving Latin novels – Petronius' *Satyrica* and Apuleius' *Metamorphoses* – suggesting that we should distinguish between the idealising texture of the Greek texts and their more bawdy, grotesque Latin equivalents. In recent years, however, increasing attention has been given to a wide range of other prose fiction texts which do not survive in full – some of them summarised in detail in the writing of the ninth-century bishop Photius, others surviving as fragments on papyrus scrolls dug up in Egypt – which expand and in some cases complicate our understanding of the novelistic writing of this period. For example the two non-surviving novels summarised by Photius – Antonius Diogenes' *Wonders Beyond Thule* and Iamblichos' *Babylonian Story* – have plots apparently even more labyrinthine than Heliodorus', and even more full of implausible moments of mistaken identity and bizarre descriptions of strange lands. Iamblichos too, like Heliodorus, identifies himself as a foreigner, and thus positions his work on the edge of Greek culture. The fragments of Lollianos' *Phoenician Story* seem to contain descriptions of loss of virginity and ritual cannibalism. In that sense Lollianos seems much closer to the content we find in Apuleius and Petronius, and backs up the impression I have argued for above, that the Greek prose fiction writers of the Roman Empire were fascinated, just like their Latin counterparts, by the pleasures of juxtaposing idealised descriptions of elite virtue with more grotesque and sensationalistic content. Apuleius himself was a practising sophist, writing and performing in both Latin and Greek, and his novel shows signs of close knowledge of the Greek novel texts, another indication that we should not separate Greek and Latin prose fiction too firmly.

Fiction outside the novels

I also want to suggest, finally, that a full picture of the Greek prose fiction of the Roman Empire needs to take account of the way in which the narrative conventions and preoccupations outlined here flow out beyond the boundary of the 'novel' genre as it has conventionally been defined, into satirical, rhetorical and biographical writing. Speeches often included narrative, as I mentioned towards the beginning of this chapter. One oration by Dio of Prusa – his *Euboian Oration* (*Oration* 7) examined in more depth in Chapter 3 – takes that tendency to a new level, starting with a long, novelistic first-person account of his shipwreck on the island of Euboia, and the hospitality he received in a rustic community there cut off from urban civilisation (that account seems to have influenced Longus), before switching in the second half to more moralising reflections. This is an age which was fascinated by exploring the new possibilities of narrative in prose, and obsessed with reflecting on the relation between truth and fiction. It was also an age with a new self-consciousness about the functions of fiction, and the relations between fiction and truth. Lucian, who is the main subject of the chapter which follows, takes that play with truth and fiction furthest of all. His *True Stories* – a parody of implausible travellers' tales like those we find in the *Odyssey* or in the work of the historian Herodotus, including a trip to the moon and encounters with tribes of flying vegetables – was an important model for Swift's *Gulliver's Travels*. Lucian early on in the work makes the claim that 'this is the only thing I will tell the truth about – the fact that I am lying' (*True Stories* 4). That claim undermines both the veracity and the moral usefulness of the prose fiction traditions Lucian is imitating.

Novelistic narrative in early Christian culture

The other direction one might look is towards early Christian literature. Much early Christian narrative is strikingly close to the ancient novels in terms of its basic plot patterns. That goes for many of the early Christian martyr acts (often grisly celebrations of the torture and death of Christian saints) and saints' lives, and indeed for the canonical New Testament Acts of the Apostles. But most relevant here are the Apocryphal Acts – stories of the apostles which were not included in the canonical New Testament, but which seem to have been widely read throughout early Christian culture, and as far as we can tell taken by many, despite their flirtation with comic and sensationalistic themes, as sincere inspirations to Christian faith. Most of these texts date from the same period as the novels already discussed. They regularly include travel to distant lands and gruesome descriptions of the threats and tortures faced by the apostles. There are reasons to think, moreover, that the influence is a two-way one, and that some of the Greek and Latin novels themselves show an awareness of Christian narrative. There are, for example, empty tomb scenes in both Chariton (3.3) and Xenophon of Ephesus (3.9) which may be intended as imitations of the Christian gospels. Often we see novelistic plot motifs being rewritten in Christian narrative for their new Christian message, made respectable by their Christian framework. For example, one repeated motif sees wives converted to Christianity by the apostles and refusing thereafter to sleep with their husbands. These scenes of conversion are in a number of cases described with the novelistic language of passionate love, with the apostles as objects of the women's desiring gaze – except that what they desire is not sexual satisfaction but the message of faith which the apostles bring – and the jilted husbands are cast as predatory seducer figures like those who threaten the heroes and heroines of the novels. In perhaps the most gruesome text of all, the *Acts of Andrew and Matthias*, those two apostles visit a city of cannibals who make a habit of capturing strangers, imprisoning them and feeding them on grass, and then killing them and putting them through a blood-extracting machine in the middle of the city so that they can be distributed as food to all the inhabitants of the city. Here as so often the apostles resist torture – in much the same way as the hero and heroine resist torture in the Greek novels – and win through in the end. This sensationalistic, bloodthirsty account is made respectable, of course, by its Christian message when the cannibals are all finally converted. But it is hard to avoid the feeling that the text is also flirting with a much less virtuous kind of appeal, imitating the Greek novels in their tendency to offer sensationalistic narrative disguised beneath a thin veneer of respectability.

Chapter 2

Satire

Lucianic 'satire'

This chapter has just one star, the second-century author Lucian. It should be said straight away that he is an uncategorisable author, perhaps more so than any of the other figures in this book: the label of satire is a poor attempt to pigeon-hole him. There is, for one thing, no word for 'satire' in Greek (just as there is no word for 'novel'). Nor does the term 'satire', with its modern connotations of comic commentary on contemporary news items, do justice to the subtleness and variety of his work. His writing cannibalises and subverts at one time or another pretty much all of the different genres discussed in this book. For example he is repeatedly interested in reshaping techniques of philosophical dialogue, inherited ultimately from Plato's accounts of the philosophical conversations of Socrates. Many of his works take the form of sophistic display speeches, of the type discussed further in Chapter 3: it seems that he spent at least some of his career performing as an orator. He engages repeatedly with the novelistic trends of fiction writing discussed in Chapter 1. He engages also with historiographical trends and traditions: one of his works is a diatribe directed against contemporary practices in the writing of history; another text, *On the Syrian Goddess*, pastiches Herodotean dialect to describe Syrian religious rituals which the author claims to have participated in. He also writes biography, both praising and denouncing a range of contemporary philosophical and religious figures (more on that in Chapter 7). In addition much of his work has an autobiographical, self-dramatising character, in the sense that he makes regular appearances as a character in his own works – although often under an assumed name and usually in ways which make it very difficult to know anything for certain about his life. That challenge is made more difficult by the fact that there is almost no mention of him within the work of his contemporaries, although it is clear from his own writing that he was born and brought up in the province of Syria (in the city of Samosata), on the very edges of the Greek-speaking world. He regularly draws attention to his own marginal position in relation to Greek culture, painting it as a factor which allows him to comment all the more authoritatively on the absurdities of Greek tradition.

Despite the variety of his work, however, I want to suggest that the word satire is not an entirely useless label. For one thing it reminds us of Lucian's influence over modern traditions of satirical writing from the Renaissance onwards: authors like Erasmus, Pope and Swift all admired and imitated Lucian's work. It also usefully raises questions about Lucian's relationship with Latin satire: in some ways, despite very significant differences, he is close to his Latin counterparts in tone and content. For example, many of his satires rely on first-person speakers who seem to be acting as masks for Lucian's own view, but who turn out on closer inspection to be guilty of many of the failings they criticise, or else in some ways complicit in the social problems to which they draw attention. Recent scholarship in Latin has argued for similar effects in the work of Juvenal, where the anger of the satirical speaker is an object of satire as much as the things he attacks. Many of the satirical depictions of drinking and dining I discuss below similarly have parallels in Latin satire. There is no particular sign that Lucian read Latin or that he drew on Latin satire. Very few Greek authors of this period admit to knowledge of Latin language or Latin literature, presumably because it was not prestigious to do so – the real renown came from their status as representatives of specifically Greek traditions dating right back to the classical period. More plausible is the possibility that both are influenced by shared models. Satire is often viewed within modern classical scholarship as a Latin invention, partly on the authority of a famous passage of Quintilian (*Institutio oratoria* 10.1.93) which makes that claim. There was, however, a parallel Greek tradition of 'Menippean' satirical writing, which followed the work of the Hellenistic Cynic writer Menippus, whose work was characterised by the interweaving of prose with inserted passages of verse. Lucian aligns himself closely with that tradition (although not with the tradition of inserted verse: some verse compositions ascribed to Lucian do survive, but there are not many examples of inserted verse within his prose works). We shall see below that he sometimes includes Menippus as a character in his dialogues, as a mask for his own satirical voice. Menippean satire also had some influence over Latin literature. The Latin antiquarian of the second century BCE, Varro, wrote a set of Menippean satires, to take just one example; Petronius' *Satyrica*, with its description of the lavish dinner party of Trimalchio, is in the same tradition; and it is clear that Latin verse satirists like Juvenal and (especially) Horace were aware of that Menippean model, although they seem to have relied on it less heavily than Lucian, and developed it in rather different directions.

Viewing the present through the past

What, then, is Lucian satirising (if anything)? To what extent is his satire directed at recognisable targets in the world around him? Some of Lucian's works take on contemporary targets, set clearly in the Roman present: for example his *Nigrinus* or *On Salaried Posts*, both of which comment unfavourably on the subservient relationship of Greek intellectuals to the wealth and power of Rome. Much of Lucian's other writing, however, is set in the distant past, often in classical Athens, offering ostentatiously unrealistic caricatures of iconic intellectual figures from the distant past. Elsewhere, Lucian seems mainly interested in playing ingenious literary games, rewriting mythical stories or pastiching important works from the classical heritage. His interest in the past and the literature of the past is partly a response to the prestige and fascination these things held for his contemporaries. This was a society proud of its own continuity with the glorious heritage of classical Greece. Lucian loves exposing the inherent absurdities and internal inconsistencies of the traditions on which that pride is based.

The atmosphere of fantasy in so much of his work also finds a more specific explanation in the idioms of contemporary rhetoric. As we saw briefly in the previous chapter, the exercise of declamation, which was used to train young orators from school level onwards in both Greek and Roman education, commonly required speakers to construct imaginary speeches for imaginary situations, often set in the distant past. The scenarios of this fantasy world of sophistry seem to have been used at least sometimes as vehicles for thinking through contemporary concerns. Thus when Lucian shows us the sixth-century BCE Athenian legislator Solon and his contemporary the Scythian wise-man Anacharsis debating the value of athletic education in the gymnasium in his *Anacharsis*, it is clear that he is using that archaising framework as a vehicle for exposing the absurdities of his contemporary world. Athletic education was still in the second century a key component of higher education in the Greek cities of the east, and attracted vast investments of time and energy from the elites of these cities, despite being viewed by some as anachronistic and irrelevant to the needs of present-day political life.

One of the techniques Lucian regularly uses to achieve that questioning of Greek tradition is the technique – familiar also from modern comedy – of literalising metaphors, taking the images and ideas which are most valued within contemporary stereotypes of the Greek heritage, and pushing them to their logical and absurd conclusions. In the work just mentioned, for example, Anacharsis, takes a literal-minded and sarcastic approach to Solon's claim that athletic education, and indeed the education offered by Greek drama, prepares the young men of Athens for bravery on the battlefield:

> Presumably, then, you will wear the armour of the comedians and tragedians, and if an attack is made against you you will put on those wide-mouthed helmets, in order to be more frightening to your opponents and to scare them; and presumably you will put on those high actors' shoes; for they will be light to run away in, if that is necessary, and if you end up pursuing the enemy, those shoes will be hard to escape from, for they will allow you take enormous strides in pursuit of them. (*Anacharsis* 31)

The idea that Athenian theatre somehow contributes to the well being of the city of Athens – and indeed that it still has some usefulness for the Greek cities even at the time when Lucian is writing, many centuries after its original composition – is here tested out to its logical conclusions, with absurd results, in the image of tragic actors attempting to scare the enemy away in battle by dressing in their stage costumes. We shall see further examples of Lucian's literal-minded humour below.

Debunking philosophers in the *Icaromenippus* and *Symposium*

At this point I want to pause and look in more depth at one particular target of Lucian's mockery – philosophers – in order to explore those problems more fully. Here especially Lucian's satire has uncomfortable implications for the intellectual life of his contemporary society, but those implications tend to be difficult to decipher for precisely the reason stated above, that is their setting within a fantasy landscape of the distant past. Let us look first at Lucian's *Icaromenippus*. Lucian's alter ego in this work is Menippus himself. We see him at the beginning of the work in conversation with a friend, explaining how his disillusionment with the hypocrisy of philosophers led him to undertake a journey into the sky, cutting off one wing from a vulture and one from an eagle and strapping them on to his arms so that he can fly up to the moon and from there to heaven. There he provokes a debate where Zeus secures the agreement of the gods for a plan to annihilate all the philosophers with lightning. The scathing tone of the work's representation of philosophers is hard to miss. But how can we possibly anchor such an apparently frivolous work within Lucian's contemporary intellectual landscape?

One answer is that the terms of Lucian's attack – focused in particular on the hypocrisy and pretension of these figures – are a (highly exaggerated, literal-minded) version of criticisms one might make against the intellectual culture of the second century. That effect of exaggeration may become clearer through a closer look at the language Menippus uses in describing his disillusionment, which arises when he approaches the philosophers for an explanation of the mysteries of the universe:

> So I chose the best of them, as far as it was possible to judge from the sullenness of their faces and the paleness of their skin and the length of their beards, for they all appeared to me at once to be very tall-talking and very high-thinking men; and putting myself in their hands, and having paid at once a considerable sum of money, and having agreed to pay the rest later when I had reached the end of my education in wisdom, I asked to be taught how to be a star-gazer and to learn the order of the universe. But far from releasing me from my former ignorance they actually threw me into further confusion, drenching me every day with 'first causes' and 'final causes', 'atoms' and 'voids', 'materials' and 'concepts' and other such things. The hardest thing for me was that although none of them agreed with any of the others and all their claims were inconsistent and contradictory, they nevertheless expect me to believe them, and each of them tried to win me over to his own doctrine. (*Icaromenippus* 5)

Several features of Lucian's scathing representation of philosophers here are typical of his work as a whole. He is fascinated, for example, by the mismatch between appearance – their stereotypically philosophical beards, and their pallor caused by too much time thinking in the shade – and underlying identity. He is also aware of the way in which different philosophical groups compete with each other in the intellectual marketplace, each advertising loudly its own distinctive opinions, while being unified by the underlying similarity of their ineffectiveness and vacuousness.

Of course those claims are not just exaggerated attacks on second-century philosophy; they also take us back to the world of Aristophanes' late fifth-century BCE comedy *Clouds*, where the old man Strepsiades goes to the 'thinking-school' of Socrates and is horrified by Socrates' pedantry and charlatanism, which are described in very similar terms. Lucian, in much the same way as Aristophanes, delights in the fantasy of debunking philosophical pedantry and turning it back on itself. He draws our attention, for example, to the philosophers' love of speculating on the causes of lightning and thunder, and on the nature of the moon. In the second half of the dialogue they get their come-uppance: the moon complains to Lucian about the fact that she is always being looked at by philosophers and misinterpreted; Lucian then passes on that complaint to Zeus, who arranges for their destruction by the very lightning and thunder which Menippus originally hoped they would be able to explain. Here the fantasy of wiping out philosophical absurdities is carried to a comically literal-minded extreme.

Those techniques of literalisation are integral to the work in other areas too. Lucian returns several times in the passage just quoted to the language of 'airiness', the habit of 'up-in-the-air' thinking. The Greek adjective *meteôros* means 'in the air', and is a term for serious study of astronomy (often in the neuter plural form *ta meteôra* – 'things in the air'), but also has a variety of metaphorical uses: it can mean 'absent-minded' or 'puffed-up'. Aristophanes in his *Clouds* literalises the language of *ta meteôra* by showing Socrates lifted up in the air in a basket in order to contemplate the heavens and to converse with the clouds, whom he takes as divinities. Lucian takes that literalisation of metaphor very much further: disgusted with the failure of the philosophers' 'airy' knowledge, he decides to replace it by literal flight, up to the moon and beyond, trumping their more contemptible versions of aerial thinking (here he also draws on Aristophanes' *Birds*, where two disillusioned Athenians found a city of the birds in the sky, blocking out the smoke of sacrifice from rising up to the gods in heaven). Menippus accordingly uses the language of airiness repeatedly himself for his own flight. Lucian plays the same game in his *True Stories*: that narrative similarly includes a trip to the moon, which literalises, in an absurd manner, philosophical allegories of the ascent of the soul.

Lucian's attack on philosophical hypocrisy is repeated in similar terms, and with similar techniques of literalisation, in his *Symposium*. The Greek symposium (drinking-party) had been a traditional space for elite interaction right back to archaic and classical Greece. In the early fourth century BCE Plato's *Symposium* – an account of Socrates and various companions discussing the nature of love at a drinking party – had established a tradition of setting learned, philosophical discussion in the symposium. Many writers of the Roman Empire follow that lead. Plutarch and Athenaeus, for example, devote long works to recording erudite drinking-party conversations (discussed further in Chapter 5). Lucian subverts that tradition brilliantly. His symposium is a wedding feast. A wide range of eminent philosophers have been invited, one representing each of the main philosophical schools. As in the *Icaromenippus*, the philosophers have all the outward trappings of their calling, but their hypocrisy and absurdity is soon exposed, when they start brawling with each other over dinner:

> Zenothemis, I tell you, ignored the bird in front of him and picked up the one in front of Hermon, which was, as I said before, fatter. Hermon, however, grabbed hold of it himself and refused to allow Zenothemis to be greedy. At this point there was a shout, and they fell on each other and hit each other in the face with the birds themselves, and grabbing hold of each other's beards they called out for help … (*Symposium* 43).

Here beards are once again important: ostensibly a badge of philosophical identity, they come to act as vehicles for the battle, making it easier for these fake intellectuals to be quite literally dragged into combat. At this point a range of other philosophers joins in. Each of them prides himself on his own philosophical allegiance, so much so that they stay in philosophical character as they fight. But of course the underlying effect is to show that they are all ultimately the same – their difference is skin-deep. Here, too, literalisation of metaphor is important: the symposium had always been a place for 'competitive' speech and playful debate; and the philosophy of the Roman Empire was, as we shall see in Chapter 4, deeply competitive, heavily interested in debate between rival belief-systems. Lucian turns that figurative sympotic, philosophical combat into something literal, and in the process he imports the Homeric language of the battlefield, which is absurdly out of place within this archetypally philosophical space. For example, two of the other philosophers fight over a bird in much the same way, and are described 'as if they were tugging at the body of Patroclus' (42).

Satirical viewing

Both these works are also intensely interested in the theme of looking, another common Lucianic preoccupation. In the *Icaromenippus*, Lucian looks down from the moon on the follies of humankind beneath him with a special kind of satirical gaze. That gaze combines a sense of distance, which makes the things below him seem minuscule and correspondingly insignificant, and an ability to focus in on the smallest details which would normally remain hidden. When he first arrives on the moon he has only the first, distant type of vision, but the philosopher Empedocles whom he meets there explains that he can gain the other type of zoom-vision too if he flaps just one of his wings, the wing of the eagle, which is a proverbially far-sighted bird. The detached, omniscient viewing of the follies of humanity which results from Empedocles' advice appropriates the position of the divine onlooker, able to uncover the most private moments of wrongdoing:

> I saw Hermodoros the Epicurean perjuring himself for the sake of a thousand drachmas, Agathokles the Stoic taking one of his pupils to court over his fees, the orator Kleinias stealing a bowl from the temple of Asklepios, and the Cynic Herophilos sleeping in a brothel. (*Icaromenippus* 16)

For the *Symposium*, too, this pose of detached viewing is crucial (as Bracht Branham has shown – see Further reading). The narrator tells us that he was not involved with the fighting: 'as for me I stood upright against the wall and watched everything without getting mixed up in it' (45). Meanwhile the fighting philosophers themselves are objects of surveillance. In a sense that is quite appropriate to the symposium: the symposium is supposed to be a time of openness, where individuals reveal their true characters under the sociable influence of wine, and where everyone is equally on view. The problem is that the philosophers do not seem to realise they are being watched. Conversely, Lucian's alter ego, the first-person narrator Lykinos, seems to feel he can get away with being a detached observer without being looked at himself (a very un-sympotic assumption). Early in the work, for example, Kleodemos the Peripatetic leans over to the Platonist Ion pointing out the bad table manners of the Stoic Zenothemis:

> 'Look how he stuffs himself with tasty food, how he has covered his cloak with soup, and how much food he hands to his servant standing behind him, thinking that he is unobserved by everyone else, and not remembering those who are eating with him. Point it out to Lykinos, so that he can bear witness to it.' But I didn't need Ion to point it out to me, for I had seen it from my vantage point (*ek periopês*) a long time before. (*Symposium* 11)

Lucian here again stresses his dispassionate, detached relationship with those he criticises, looking on coolly, with all the social dynamics of the symposium in view, watching Kleodemos and Ion watching Zenothemis (although the fact that Kleodemos and Ion address him with such easy familiarity might lead us to wonder whether he is quite so easily separated from these false philosophers as he claims to be).

Greek intellectuals and Roman patrons: *On Salaried Posts*

The difficulty for modern readers, of course – accustomed as we are to forms of satire which attack their subjects explicitly, for example by tying comic commentary to specific recent news events – is that it is still hard to see how these works can be said to be targeting anything beyond a generalised view of the vanity of philosophical pretensions. The question remains: would Lucian's readers really have recognised these works as having any relevance to the world of the second century? There are, however, a number of representations of philosophers in Lucian's work which are more clearly set in the present day. In particular his *On Salaried Posts* offers another fascinating rewriting of the traditions of the literary symposium, and a fascinating rethinking of some of the images of Plato's version.

The work describes the experience of a Greek intellectual employed as a member of the household of a wealthy Roman, and the various degradations and humiliations that involves. The intellectual in question has dreams of gaining wealth and respect through the position, but finds from his very first dinner invitation onwards that quite the opposite is true:

> Having bathed and put on clean clothes and having prepared your-self as elegantly as possible you arrive at the dinner party, afraid of arriving before the others: for it is uncouth to do so, just as it is boorish to arrive late. So having waited (*têrêsas*) for the very middle of the best arrival period you enter, and your host welcomes you very respectfully and someone ushers you in and gives you a place just above the rich man with perhaps two of his old friends. But you, as if you have entered the home of Zeus, are amazed (*tethaumakas*) by everything and excited (lit. 'up in the air' (*meteôros*)) by every-thing which is going on: for all of this is foreign to you and unfamiliar. And the servants look at you (*apoblepei*) and everyone who is present looks (*epitêrousin*) at what you are doing, nor is this something the rich host neglects, but he has actually instructed some of his servants to watch (*episkopein*) how you look (*apoblepseis*) at his wife or his concubines from your vantage-point (*ek periôpes*). The attendants of the other guest, seeing (*horôntes*) you so astonished, mock at your inexperience of proceedings, taking as proof of your never having dined with anyone else before the fact that your napkin is new. (*On Salaried Posts* 14-15)

What follows is an uncomfortable description of the physical discomfort of the experience, and the vicious carping of his fellow-guests, envious of the fact that the intellectual has been given a more prestigious seat at dinner than them. Roman drinking-party traditions tended to be more blatantly hierarchical, in contrast with the Greek sympotic stress on equality: on one level what we are seeing here is a clash between Greek expectations and Roman reality.

The unnamed intellectual falls short of his sophisticated aspirations in a great range of ways, marked out by Lucian's rewriting here of the traditions of the symposium genre. The first sentence of this extract, for example, echoes the opening pages of Plato's *Symposium*, where we hear that Socrates, uncharacteristically, had bathed and put on shoes before attending the party (174a). That echo casts the intellectual as a Socrates figure, but the second half of the sentence undercuts that aspiration cruelly: Socrates had famously arrived late at the banquet of Agathon, having stood motionless outside the door thinking for some time (174e-175d). By contrast, this intellectual's anxiety over the niceties of social convention is about as far removed from that freedom as imaginable. The mockery of the servants also has similar implications: playful teasing of one's fellow-guests had always been a staple feature of symposium culture, but to be mocked by servants is a degrading alternative.

In addition the language of looking is once again omnipresent here (as Tim Whitmarsh has demonstrated – see Further reading) (and as the Greek words noted in brackets in the passage quoted above make clear). The intellectual is himself on the alert: he 'watches out' (*têrêsas*) for the right moment to go in; and he gazes in astonishment (*tethaumakas*) at what he sees. At first it seems to be the case that his awed and respectful looking is being returned in kind: we hear that the servants looked at him (*apoblepei*), which might at first be taken as a sign of their solicitude. But as that sentence proceeds it becomes clear that we have a much more sinister kind of looking, designed to judge and test the intellectual's suitability. He may imagine himself able to look around the room in a detached fashion from the vantage-point (*ek periôpes* – the same phrase used for Lykinos detached looking in *Symposium* 11, quoted above) of his couch, but in fact he is himself being watched in turn: the Lucianic fantasy of detached viewing is not so easy to maintain. The sense of the intellectual being sucked in to this new and humiliating world intensifies in what follows: Lucian goes so far as to describe this as a kind of willing slavery, an example of the selling of philosophy, a process he mocks repeatedly elsewhere. Of course the intellectual himself is one of the objects of mockery in this work. Nevertheless Lucian's constant use of the second person challenges us to see ourselves in his plight and to consider the possibility that it is not so easy to separate ourselves from the absurdities of philosophical hypocrisy which he mocks in his *Sympo-sium*; indeed Lucian in another work, his *Apology*, admits to the fact that some people might accuse him of hypocrisy when they read his *On Salaried Posts*, given that he has subsequently accepted an administrative position in Egypt – although he tries hard to argue that the two cases are not comparable.

Assessing *paideia*

Lucian's interest in contemporary intellectual and cultural life goes far beyond philosophy, but one of the things which unifies it is the fact that it is saturated with an awareness of the importance of *paideia* ('learning', 'education') as a badge of high status. He mocks those who take the contemporary obsession with erudition to extremes, or who use it in too pretentious a fashion. Many orators were keen 'atticisers', in other words they performed in the dialect of fifth-century Athens, using vocabulary quite alien to the day-to-day spoken Greek of the Roman Empire. Lucian himself has a wonderful command over Attic Greek and is often held up as a supreme example of it; he also loves obscure vocabulary himself. In his *Lexiphanes*, however, he turns the tables, attacking an individual whose use of archaising vocabulary is taken to extremes: the man is depicted vomiting up the rare words with which he has stuffed himself. And in his *Ignorant Book-Collector* he attacks an unnamed man for the fact the he has accumulated a costly library but is too ignorant to under-stand the books it contains. That attack on empty pretension is similar in character to the attacks on philosophers we have seen already. In two other works, the *Alexander* and *On the Death of Peregrinus* – both of which have biographical tendencies, discussed in more depth in Chapter 7 – he attacks two contemporary figures who have preyed on the gullibility of the common people in order to gain a reputation not only as philosophers but also as sages and miracle-workers (the boundaries between philo-sophical and religious activity were more fluid than they are for us).

Not all his works are critical, however – at times Lucian chooses to praise and defend. His *Demonax* praises a contemporary philosophical figure, and consists of a long accumulation of anecdotes to demonstrate Demonax's wisdom and witty sayings. Another work, *On the Dance*, is a defence of the art of 'pantomime', a form of dance which was highly popular, but which also attracted much disapproval for its erotic over-tones. Lucian's case (or rather the case of his *alter ego* in the dialogue, Lykinos, whose opinions do not necessarily match Lucian's own views straightforwardly) paints pantomime, with typically sophistic ingenuity, as an ancient art which plays a central part in Greek mythical tradition and which matches the skills of the rhetorician. He even goes so far as to link the origins of dance with the creation of the universe: '... those who recount its genealogy most truthfully would tell you that dance came into being together with the first origins of the universe, making its appearance together with the ancient god Eros [i.e. the god of love]. For the dancing of the stars and the interweaving of the wandering planets with the fixed stars, and their rhythmic partnership and well-ordered harmony are all evidence for this primordial dance' (*On the Dance* 7). We do know that some ancient commentators worked hard to present pantomime as an elevated and respectable art form. Lucian takes that process to extremes, drawing on the common sophistic rhetorical exercise of giving speeches in defence of objects which one would usually find it hard to defend. In the process he hints at links between his own sophistic skills of crowd-pleasing self-dramatisation and the dancer's flamboyant powers of mimicry and spectacle (as Ismene Lada-Richards has argued – see Further reading).

Eavesdropping on the gods

My focus so far has been on tracing some of the contemporary resonances of Lucian's work, apparent even within more fantastical works like the *Symposium* and the *Icaromenippus*. I have suggested that one of the unifying features of his work is his love of exposing intellectual pretension, hypocrisy and inconsistency. However, we should not be too solemn about insisting on these aims of social criticism. The word 'satire' is after all our term for Lucian's writing, not his own, and there are some works where it seems particularly inappropriate, where we would do better to concentrate on appreciating Lucian's virtuoso mastery of the sophistic skills of reimagining traditional stories in ingenious new ways. One of the best – and funniest – examples is a set of four works with broadly similar character: *Dialogues of the Gods*, *Dialogues of the Sea Gods*, *Dialogues of Courtesans* and *Dialogues of the Dead*. In these texts, each of which contains a range of miniature dialogues, Lucian imagines mythical and historical figures in conversation, discussing their concerns in often mundane fashion. One of the recurring pleasures which the literature of this period offers is the opportunity for the reader or listener to have access to the voices of the past – to hear the tones of the great classical orator Demosthenes reincarnated in the speech of a sophist, or to enter into a kind of virtual debate with the great sages of the past within the period's great volume of encyclopaedic and miscellanistic writing, discussed further in Chapter 5. That is the pleasure Lucian taps into in these four works. Here again the technique of literalisation, of following common stories and images to their logical conclusions, imagining what things would really be like if the stories were true, is a key source of Lucian's humour. In *Dialogues of the Gods* 18, for example, Hera berates Zeus for the behaviour of his son Dionysus (a god associated with ecstatic, eastern religion): Dionysus has gone off the rails, she says, hanging around with mad women and tying his hair up with ribbons; in 12, Aphrodite scolds her son Eros in the language of a neurotic parent, for always making the gods fall in love with mortals, but Eros quietens her by threatening to stop Ares from being in love with her; in 26, Apollo complains to Hermes that he finds it very hard to tell apart the twins Castor and Pollux now that they have been given the gift of immortality, although with the requirement that they must not be in Olympus at the same time.

Unreliable narration in the *True Stories*

That fantasy of access to voices usually buried within the mythical tradition recurs repeatedly elsewhere in Lucian's work. It is present, for example, in the *Icaromenippus*, in the scenes of Lucian's encounter with the gods. In another brief work, the *Conversation with Hesiod*, Lucian quizzes the ancient poet about whether he lied in his poetry about the promises given to him by the Muses. And in Lucian's *True Stories*, Lucian himself is entertained on the Isles of the Blessed, the home of deceased Greek heroes, and has the opportunity to question Homer about his work:

> Among other things I asked him where he was from, saying that even to this day that point was much debated in our society. He said that he was not unaware of the fact that some people said he was from Chios, some from Smyrna, and many from Kolophon; however he said that he was himself a Babylonian, and that his name among his fellow-citizens was not Homer but Tigranes, and that he had changed his name later when held hostage (*homêreusas*) by the Greeks ... In addition I was eager to know this as well, if he had written the *Odyssey* before the *Iliad*, as most people say. He said that he hadn't ... And I often used to do this at other times afterwards, if I ever saw that he was at leisure, going up to him and asking him questions ... (*True Stories* 2.20)

In typically Lucianic fashion this passage throws doubt on the Greekness of Greek tradition: Homer, one of the great icons of Greek heritage, turns out to be a barbarian. It also debunks the industry of debate which had grown up around Homer's work. Homer's birthplace was genuinely disputed and many cities laid claim to it in order to enhance their own prestige. Lucian represents himself as able to cut through all of the scholarly debates surrounding the poems with a new authority, on the basis of personal contact with Homer. That said – and with a typical Lucianic twist – it is also clear that the first-person narrator is himself an absurd figure in some ways. Elsewhere in the text, for example, we see that he is a troublesome intruder in the Isles of the Blessed. It is tempting to feel here that Homer's heart sinks every time Lucian approaches, and perhaps even that the responses he offers are designed simply to get rid of his questioner at the first opportunity. Certainly his replies have an air of bathos, not least in his one word response to the relative priority of his two poems. Perhaps Lucian's account is not so reliable as he claims.

The *True Stories* is in fact Lucian's most famous and most extended play with the figure of the unreliable narrator. Most often quoted is the opening section of the work, already discussed in Chapter 1, where he denounces lying narrators. His own story, he says, will be different:

> This is the only thing I will tell the truth about – the fact that I am lying … Thus I am writing about things I have neither seen nor experienced nor heard from anyone else, things which are further-more entirely non-existent and which could never come into being in the first place. For that reason those who read this book should not believe it at all. (*True Stories* 1.4)

Similarly in his *Lover of Lies*, Lucian denounces the habit of telling lying stories for the sake of it, illustrated through a set of fantastical tales which reveal the attractions of lying narrative even as they are used to denounce it. In the *True Stories*, he imitates among others the narrative voice of Odysseus, picking up on the impression ingrained both within the *Odyssey*, and in later tradition, of Odysseus as an unreliable and tricky narrator who distorts the story of his travels for his own ends. Lucian's account seems to confirm that impression when Odysseus sidles up to him just as he is leaving the Isles of the Blessed and asks him to take a letter to the goddess Calypso, telling her that he very much regrets his decision not to accept her offer of immortality, and that he plans to give his wife Penelope the slip at the earliest opportunity and come and join her (2.29 and 2.35-6). The difference between the Odysseus of the *Odyssey* and Lucian's narra-tor in the *True Stories* is that the self-aggrandisement of the latter is more blatant and more transparent. These effects of unreliable narration are one of the key features of Lucian's work, and one of their consequences is to challenge us as readers. If we trust Lucian's narrating voices too much, if we go along with his first-person judgements on the absurdity of human society, if we lose sight of the fact that the narrating voice is itself an object of satire too, we end up at risk of falling into absurdity ourselves. Nobody is safe from absurdity in Lucianic satire, least of all the reader. Even the apparently straightforward claim about the falsity of the *True Stories* is more complicated than it looks. It does, of course, mock implausible authors and gullible readers, but it also potentially leads us into the trap of excessive scepticism, of taking what follows as entirely frivolous, tempting us to drop our guard and so not recognise the way in which the work debunks the idealisation of traditional literature in which all of Lucian's readers would have been to one degree or another been complicit.

One might see all of this as a comment on techniques of fictionalisation in this period – not just novelistic fictionalisation, but also fictionalisation in other fields of literary production. Lucian mocks the pose of authoritative, realistic narration. He pokes fun at allegorical representations of truth in philosophical writing. He also draws attention to the artificiality of his own first-person voice. That kind of constructedness was important for the literary and sophistic voices of this period, as we shall see in Chapter 3. Once again, however, we should not be too solemn, nor should we underestimate the degree to which Lucian revels in his status as a virtuoso exponent of precisely the systems of communication he debunks: the skills of self-fictionalisation and ingenious rewriting of tradition. There is perhaps no other ancient author who developed those skills to such a high level. They are skills which still form key resources in modern comedy (though not necessarily in modern 'satire' as we understand that term). Lucian's continuing appeal for modern readers is remarkable: despite the fact that his work is so rooted in the sophistic idioms of his own time there is surely no other ancient author whose work has had so many affinities with modern humour, and so much influence over it.

Chapter 3

Oratory

The role of sophistic oratory in the Roman period

It would be easy, on the basis of the material we have looked at so far, to underestimate the difficulty and rigour of much Imperial Greek literature. The oratorical texts we will look at in this chapter, and the philosophical and scientific texts of Chapters 4 and 5, are often very difficult to read. They are the products of the very highest level of sophisticated and painstaking educational processes which demanded great commitment from their practitioners. Not only the great sophistic orators of this period, but also those who were put through a rhetorical education at a much lower level, devoted vast amounts of time to repetitive training exercises which allowed them to master the necessary skills to stand before a critical audience and perform, often improvising, with all the linguistic skill and physical confidence expected of them. At its best, sophistic oratory was enormously popular: Philostratus paints the sophists as charismatic fig-ures who could charm huge crowds with the magic of their tongues. But a first look at the speeches themselves as they survive on paper can sometimes leave us disappointed, curious about what the contemporaries of the sophists might have seen in their performances.

What, then, makes the Greek oratory of the Roman world different from what had come before? Many of its features are entirely typical of the role of oratory in other times and places. Oratory had formed a key plank of ancient education for many centuries in both Greek and Latin. Command over the skills of persuasive speaking had been important for the politicians of classical Athens or Republican Rome, and even within the Homeric poems we see early representations of the importance of debating skill for heroes like Achilles and Agamemnon. Oratory had throughout that time been a skill which conferred great prestige, but also a skill which sometimes attracted negative representations, linked with deception and trickery. That worry about the moral status of rhetoric had been one reason for the hostility directed against the first sophists – the new intellectuals of classical Greece, whose claim to be able to 'make the weaker argument the stronger' (as famously claimed by the sophist

Protagoras) is treated in negative terms by writers as varied as Aristophanes and Plato. Much of that ambivalence was still in evidence for
Imperial Greek culture, as we shall see.

It does seem to be the case, however, that the relative prestige of
different types of oratory underwent a shift in the second and third
centuries. Epideictic oratory (the oratory of praise and blame, often used
in honorific speeches) came increasingly to match the prominence of the
kinds of oratory on which the reputation of great orators of the past like
Demosthenes and Cicero had been founded: deliberative oratory (the kind
of speech-making which is aimed at influencing political policy) and
forensic (i.e. law-court) oratory (although it is important to stress that the
sophists' speeches were not only of the epideictic variety: it was common
for sophists to give imaginary deliberative speeches, recreating a situation
from the distant past and speaking in favour of a particular course of action
as if to an audience of the time). That development seems to have been
linked with a revived interest in the Greek cultural heritage: the sophists
mattered not just as people who could sway public policy or influence
legal decisions, but also as speakers whose words were to be admired for
their own sake, as representatives of the classical Greek tradition. In
addition, they were valued because they had command over the language
of honour, which on some accounts had become even more important
within the status-conscious Roman world, with the emperor at its head,
than it had been before: the sophists could confer honour through their
mastery of techniques of encomium.

The prestige of sophistry

There is a danger of overstatement, however. For one thing, it is important
to point out that the increasing interest in rhetoric in the second century
CE did not come from nowhere. It was prefigured, among other things, by
the work of the many Greek rhetoricians who were active in Rome in the
late first century BCE and early first century CE. Apollodoros of Pergamon
was the rhetor chosen by Julius Caesar to take charge of the education of the
future emperor Augustus, and his Art of Rhetoric was translated into Latin.
Along with others like Theodoros of Gadara, who taught the future emperor
Tiberius, and Dionysius of Halicarnassus, whose historical writings are
discussed briefly in Chapter 6, he made influential advances in theorising
rhetoric and cementing its place at the centre of both Greek and Roman elite
education. Philostratus, in the early sections of Book 1 of the Lives of the
Sophists, discusses the role of classical Greek orators such as Aeschines and
Gorgias as predecessors of his own contemporaries, but oddly makes no

mention of these late-Hellenistic/early-Imperial developments, presumably because they are not relevant to his focus on sophistic display oratory.

Perhaps more importantly, we need to be cautious of the assumption that the new importance of epideictic speech-making was caused by a decline in the link between rhetorical skill and the real world of politics and law. That claim risks falling in with the stereotype of Imperial Greek culture as politically disempowered and subservient to Rome. It is clear, on the contrary, that the Greek cities of the east had very active institutions of democratic debate throughout the Roman period, although they were admittedly more oligarchical in constitutional terms than the classical Athenian democracy on which they were based.

We also rely heavily on one text for our understanding of the sophists of the Roman Empire, that is Philostratus' *Lives of the Sophists*. There are reasons to think that Philostratus exaggerates the importance of his subjects: I will have more to say, in Chapter 7, about Philostratus' self-serving agenda and his rather idiosyncratic techniques of biographical characterisation. For the vast majority of 'ordinary' members of the educated Greek elite it must still have been the skills of deliberative oratory which were most useful, and which took up the bulk of education time. For these people oratory was a more mundane, less showy activity than one would imagine from having read Philostratus and nothing else. Even epideictic speech-making, in the hands of an ordinary member of the educated Greek upper classes, must have seemed like a very much less flashy affair. The rhetorical specialists most individuals would have encountered were rhetorical teachers, or 'rhetors' rather than sophists. The Greek word rhetor is used for anyone offering a rhetorical education; the word sophist is not used consistently, but most often seems to apply to a smaller subset of that group, describing anyone distinguished enough to give display speeches as well.

Still, for all their oddity, it is clear that the sophists were figures who held a broad fascination within Imperial Greek culture. Many of the details of Philostratus' account can be corroborated from other sources: the picture he paints may have exaggerations and distorting factors, but it is not fantasy. The most famous of them, men like Polemo and Herodes Atticus, the two figures who take the lion's share of Philostratus' biography, accumulated vast wealth and political influence. Herodes undertook public building on an enormous scale: he was responsible, among many other buildings, for the *odeion* (i.e. small theatre) which still stands on the south slopes of the Acropolis in Athens and which bears his name and for the athletic stadium in the east of the city, in which the 1896 Athens Olympics and some parts of the 2004 games were held. Both are portrayed by Philostratus as immensely arrogant and controversial men, as indeed are many of the other sophists. These are quasi-heroic figures, whose skills often seem to raise them above the level of ordinary mortals, and whose competitive love of glory often leads them into damaging conflicts with each other. Philostratus is fascinated above all by the voices of his subjects. He characterises each of the sophists differently according to his particular style of eloquence; he also regularly uses the language of oracular speech to describe their speech-giving, as if to stress its divinely inspired quality. Clearly the physicality of their performance also mattered: the bodily presence of the greatest sophists, their mastery of the gestures and poses which marked them out as representatives of elite masculinity, their ability to conquer the stresses and nerves of live performance – all of these things must have contributed to the fascination of these occasions (as Maud Gleason has shown – see Further reading). Philostratus tells us, too, that they were honoured as benefactors and icons of Greek culture by cities across the eastern Mediterranean, and indeed that picture is confirmed by frequent references to sophists within the epigraphical record: when Greek cities granted honours to a prominent individual they would routinely put up an inscription and sometimes also a statue to celebrate that fact. Many sophists gained these honours by serving on embassies to the emperor, asking, for example, for permission to found a new festival, or pleading the city's case in a dispute with a neighbouring community. In that situation the speaker's command of rhetoric would act as an emblem of the city's status as a representative of traditional Greek culture, and so of its fittingness to win the emperor's approval. At the same time, however, the sophists never turned their back on the day-to-day processes of rhetorical training and education: for many, a key part of their activity was the teaching of students. Philostratus accordingly tends to record the intellectual genealogy of each of his subjects, telling us at the beginning of each life which great predecessor each of his new subjects was educated under, in a way which portrays the continuation of the Greek intellectual heritage as a concrete process, passed on endlessly from teacher to pupil.

Menander Rhetor

What do we find, then, when we turn to the surviving speeches of Imperial Greek world? If we approach this material in the hope of finding the beguiling voices of sophists captured and fixed for ever on paper we are likely to be disappointed. One problem we have is that relatively few speeches survive from the most prominent of the sophists. In the case of both Polemo and Herodes Atticus, for example, hardly any surviving works have come down to us. That is partly, of course, because many sophistic speeches were improvised and not written up for publication – although we do have some evidence for stenographers taking down speeches as they were delivered. In fact much of the material we have is linked in some way or another with the processes of rhetorical education, either in the form of theoretical treatises on rhetoric, a traditional genre dating at least as far back as the work of Aristotle in the fourth century BCE, or else practice exercises, designed to give models for imitation to aspiring young orators, many of them aimed at individuals interested in the more mundane skills of functional oratory than in the mastery of high-level sophistic display. It is hardly surprising that they seem to lack the electrifying thrill which drives Philostratus' enthusiasm.

The best surviving example of these educational texts is the work of Menander Rhetor. The two treatises which have come down to us under his name (although it is not certain that both are by the same author) seem likely to have been written some time in the late third century CE. They are thus at least fifty years later than most of the other works discussed in this book, but they are not for that reason irrelevant. It is easy to think of the high period of Imperial Greek literature coming to an end after the 230s CE, when the last of Philostratus' texts seem to have been written, and it is true that there are very few if any literary masterpieces (at least if one exempts early Christian writing from the picture) surviving from the next hundred years. Within the field of oratory, however, there seems to have been a high degree of continuity right through to the Christian era, at least to the fourth century, when Libanius of Antioch emerged as one of the greatest orators and teachers in the whole history of Greek literature. Menander's approach would have seemed entirely familiar to a member of the second-century Greco-Roman elite, just as it would have done to an educated fourth-century Christian seeking to master the arts of public speaking.

The two treatises give lengthy instructions about how to give epideictic speeches in a wide range of different contexts. Treatise two, for example, offers us instructions on how to praise the emperor, how to give a speech of arrival (either addressing a visitor who has just arrived in one's home city or addressing a city one has just arrived in oneself), how to give a *lalia* (a light introductory speech, which often involved telling a story to illustrate one's point – a genre Lucian makes use of regularly), how to give a *propemptikon* (a speech of *bon voyage*), how to give a wedding speech and a bridal-chamber speech (the latter delivered outside the bedroom of the bride and groom), a birthday speech, a speech of consolation, a speech of praise to a provincial governor, a funeral speech, a crowning speech (honouring an individual being presented with a ceremonial crown in thanks for services to the city), an ambassador's speech, an invitation speech, a leaving speech, a monody (speech of lament), and a speech in honour of the god Apollo. Each of these chapters categorises the many different possibilities one might be confronted with, offering an easily accessible guide to what one should say in every eventuality. In the section on speeches of arrival, for example, we are instructed as follows:

> After this, as a second section, you will add a balanced encomium of the founder of the city himself. The third section is that in which you describe the nature of the place, how it stands in relation to sea, mainland and climate ... In the passage concerning the mainland you will describe the beauty of the plains, the rivers, the harbours and the hills; in the passage concerning the sea, you will describe how convenient it is for those who put into harbour there, and by what seas it is washed; in the passage concerning the climate you will say that it is healthy. Under each of these headings you will offer a comparison, comparing this place to another place: for example by saying that it lies in a good location, like Italy, but differs in that Italy is situated in a part of the world near to barbarians, or even at the very end of the inhabited world, whereas this place is either near to Greece or in the very middle of the inhabited world, and is more favoured by nature both in relation to the mainland and the sea. In comparing the climate, your comparison will be with the climate either of the Athenians or of the Ionians.
> (Menander Rhetor, *Treatise* 2, 383)

The methodical, prescriptive character of these instructions should be clear even from this short sample, although it is worth stressing that even this very functional text could carry an intense ideological charge, bolstering its readers' sense of the high value of their own culture. The assumptions of the geographical and cultural centrality of Greece underlying this work – and indeed the sense of a shared set of rhetorical resources and a shared Greek elite etiquette – are hard to miss.

Aelius Aristides

No doubt these examples were used as ready-made speeches by harassed local notables unsure of how to approach their own speaking engagements. However, the same conventions were also available to more talented orators, to be reshaped in highly original ways; indeed to some extent Menander's instructions represent a distillation of techniques found in great speeches of the past. We are lucky to have a number of specific examples of praise of particular cities to demonstrate that. Perhaps most famous are the speeches of Aelius Aristides in praise of Athens and in praise of Rome. In his Roman Oration, Aristides makes Rome the natural protector of Greek culture, praising the way in which the Roman Empire has offered a divinely inspired framework for the flourishing of Greek culture. In the Athens speech, which was written for the festival of the Panathenaia in honour of the goddess Athena, and so known as the *Panathenaicus*, Aristides imitates the classical orator Isocrates, who had famously argued for Athens' status as the rightful cultural leader of the Greek world in his own *Panathenaicus* many centuries before. The ingenuity with which Aristides manipulates the hellenocentric conventions of geographical praise outlined above are immediately obvious (in fact Menander Rhetor's instruction are formed partly from his reading of Aristides' work, which he mentions regularly):

> For it is situated, in preference to any other guardpost of Greece, in the proper position, as the first land facing the east, jutting out into the sea, making it clear for anyone to see that it has been made by the gods as the defender of Greece, and that to this city alone it is natural to be the leader of the Greek people. Moreover it shows signs of a sort of kindness, in that it sticks out far into the sea, taming it, and it mingles with the islands, a most pleasant sight, a mainland among the islands, and more southerly than some of these, first of all stretching out a kind of hand to welcome them, and providing all kinds of anchorages and harbours all the way round itself. (*Panathenaicus* 9-10)

And again a few paragraphs later:

> Thus although the land is the start of Greece, it is nonetheless also in the middle of all of Greece. For wherever you go from Athens, the most famous peoples of Greece will receive you ... For that reason this city alone has taken upon itself in an unblemished way the appearance of the Greeks, and is to the highest degree possible racially different from the barbarians. For to the extent that it is separated by the nature of its location, to the same extent it stands apart from the barbarians in the behaviour of its men. (14)

The difference from Menander Rhetor's more pedestrian version should be clear. This is a very complex speech, flaunting its own difficulty and extravagance; it also has an extraordinary boldness and flamboyancy of imagery, for example in the startling image of the hand of Attica reaching down into the Aegean sea in a gesture of welcome.

Favorinus

The language of praise can seem stilted to modern ears, but thinking about epideictic speeches within their particular performance contexts can often help to bring them to life. It is hard to imagine Aristides' Athenian listeners (or rather his notional Athenian listeners, if we view this as a speech which might have been revised for publication after delivery, as must often have been the case) finding anything offensive in Aristides' praise, with its seductive conjuring up of the city of Athens almost as a living being, a constant, divinely sponsored presence keeping the Greek world safe and civilised across the many centuries of its history. But there are other examples of speeches to cities which are rather more double-edged and uncomplimentary. One particularly good example is the *Corinthian Oration* of Favorinus. Favorinus was one of the most extraordinary literary figures of the second century. He was born in what is now southern France. From birth he had a medical condition – probably involving undescended testicles – which left him with a squeaky, feminine voice. The fact that he managed to master the hyper-masculine, hellenocentric world of sophistic oratory despite these twin defects – non-Greekness and effeminacy – is a sign of the transformative, empowering potential of rhetorical training as it was envisaged in the second century. In his *Corinthian Oration*, Favorinus famously explores the paradoxes of his own identity, and in the process pokes fun at his Corinthian audience, effectively comparing them with himself and so questioning their own Greek credentials. Corinth was traditionally one of the great cities of classical Greece, and the host of one of the four great athletic and musical festivals of the Greek festival calendar, the Isthmian festival, and still prided itself on those traditions. And yet it had been destroyed by the Romans in the 140s BC, and only refounded a hundred years later with many of its new inhabitants drawn from the city of Rome itself. This was not an authentic Greek city at all. The speech as a whole is a criticism of the city of Corinth for taking down a statue of Favorinus when he was thought to have fallen into disfavour with the emperor. He wraps up his address to the city in the familiar language of encomium, referring regularly to Corinth's glorious mythical past, but always in a way that makes it clear, in a rather sarcastic fashion, that the present-day city may not have lived up to that glorious heritage.

Dio of Prusa

It is difficult to know whether Favorinus' speech to the Corinthians would have seemed offensive or playful (a question further complicated by uncertainties about whether it would have been delivered in the form it has come down to us). The latter option is more likely than one might at first imagine: epideictic speech-making may well have been another space – rather like the elite symposium – where one could get away with teasing which in different contexts might be unacceptable. But in a sense that dilemma is precisely the point: the orator's voice (and here we see one obvious point of contact between Lucian and the sophists) is often double-edged, hard to read, full of tricks to trip the unwary interpreter. One particularly interesting parallel for that effect lies in theories about how to talk to kings and rulers. Menander Rhetor's instructions on praise of emperors begins with the stipulation that this kind of oration 'allows nothing ambivalent or debatable, because the person being addressed is so highly honoured' (*Treatise* 2, 368). Others, however, hint that there were acknowledged sophistic techniques of criticising while appearing to do the opposite, through the application of 'figured speech', which allowed one to hide one's real meaning behind rhetorical adornment, preserving enough 'deniability' to make it impossible for any accusation of disloyalty to stick. Dio of Prusa's 'Kingship Orations' (*Orations* 1-4) are a good example. These texts may have been delivered in front of the emperor Trajan (or at the very least they invite us to imagine them having been delivered in front of the emperor). They are striking among other things for their coerciveness: Dio sets up an idealised image of kingly virtues, with the implication that Trajan should conform to them if he wants to do his job properly, corralling Trajan into agreement with him, and so advertising the power of Greek intellectual culture to guide and watch over the emperor. At times Dio even risks rather unflattering comparisons for Trajan (as Tim Whitmarsh has demonstrated – see Further reading). In *Oration* 2, for example, he implicitly compares Trajan with Alexander the Great. The comparison has obvious appropriateness, given that Trajan was an aggressively expansionist emperor, keen on expanding the boundaries of the Empire just as Alexander had pushed back the boundaries of the Greek world. But it is hard, as Whitmarsh shows, not to see this in part as a self-serving claim for Dio's own importance, given that he draws attention to Alexander's hot-headed nature, and to the way in which it is tamed by philosophical advice and education, of the kind Dio purports to offer himself. His praise of Trajan as a 'philosophical' king is not simply a reflection of something self-evident, although it gives the impression of being so on first reading. Instead it has a note of threat and instruction: Trajan, Dio implies, must be philosophical, and must follow his instruction to become so.

The margins of sophistry

So far, then, we have seen something of the way in which epideictic conventions – mastery of which was a central part of rhetorical education – could be put to use not just in mundane and routine social rituals, but also in more elevated and sometimes double-edged form by some of the sophistic stars of the second century. There is, however, one oddity about all three of the figures I have been focusing on here – Aristides, Favorinus and Dio – and that is the fact that all three of them seem to have had quite a marginal relationship with mainstream sophistic culture as far as we can reconstruct it (the same, in fact, goes for Lucian). All three certainly avoid associating themselves with sophistry at various times. That might be explained in part by the negative connotations traditionally attached to the term 'sophist'. It may be that other 'sophists' too, if their work survived, would have been reluctant to admit to that label, preferring instead to associate themselves with other areas of intellectual expertise. Philostratus is in fact quite unusual in taking such a positive view of the term. Nevertheless there does seem to have been something different about all three of these men. Philostratus certainly seems to confirm the impression that both Favorinus (*Lives of the Sophists* 1.8) and Dio (*Lives of the Sophists* 1.7) stood apart from the other sophists in significant ways: he lists both of them as 'philosophers who were often thought to be sophists'. It may even be that for all three figures their slightly standoffish relationship to mainstream sophistic trends was one of the things which made them more inclined to self-dramatisation on paper, being less caught up with the day-to-day business of speech-making and teaching, and so more accessible to us now, reliant as we are on written sources, nearly two thousand years later.

Aelius Aristides' non-oratorical output consists of just one text, his *Sacred Tales*, a first-person diary of a chronic illness which afflicted him for many years and of his attempts to become well with the help of the god of healing, Asklepios. The diary covers many years of his life, during which time he seems to have neglected all duties of speaking and teaching. It is very far removed from the flowery, formal language of the speech quoted above. Aristides gives relentless attention to his physical symptoms, describing in great detail the dreams sent by the god and the various cures he attempted in obedience with the god's instructions. In that sense it is typical of a widespread interest in Roman Imperial literature in the relation between the human body and its underlying identity, and in the threats to identity which physical suffering brings with it: for example we have seen in Chapter 1 the prominent role given to scenes of torture of the hero and heroine in the Greek novels. Aristides charts the way in which his illness threatens his identity as an orator, preventing him from proper devotion to his rhetorical exercises and striking at the heart of the physical soundness which was almost a prerequisite for the swaggering, hyper-masculine demands of sophistic performance. In the process he forges a new identity for himself through his pain and through his narrative of that pain, an identity founded upon his relationship with the god.

But it is perhaps Dio of Prusa who goes furthest in exploring his ambivalent relationship with sophistry and rhetoric in a set of self-dram-atising speeches and narratives second only to Lucian in the inventiveness and complexity of their various masks and personas. Clearly Dio was a forceful orator. Like most of Philostratus' 'proper' sophists he was also a wealthy and controversial figure. It is clear from his own work and also from external sources (including a pair of letters on the subject between Pliny the Younger, during his time as governor of the province of Bithynia, and the emperor Trajan: Pliny, *Letters* 10.81-2) that he was accused of corruption by his fellow citizens in the city of Prusa (in modern Turkey, south of Istanbul) in relation to a public building project he had helped to fund. He was heavily involved with local politics in Prusa, but he also spoke widely in other parts of the Greek-speaking world, and many of his works are speeches of advice to specific cities. These speeches draw in many cases on the kind of epideictic traditions of civic praise already discussed for Aristides and Favorinus. Nevertheless Dio also has a stand-offish relationship to mainstream sophistry, as Philostratus recognised. That may be partly because he was active at a chronologically very early stage of the sophistic movement, in the late first and early second centuries. But there is more to it than that. His philosophical allegiances were strong, in fact his primary self-identification seems to have been as a philosopher. In the past it has often been suggested that he underwent a conversion from rhetoric to philosophy in the middle of his career, in the period of his exile by the emperor Domitian. In practice, however, it seems better to view a tension between oratory and philosophy stretching right through his career. That philosophical perspective is reflected in the speeches of advice just mentioned, which supplement their epideictic framework with moralising criticism of his target cities for their failure to safeguard and live up to Greek tradition.

Dio of Prusa, *Oration* 7

Here I examine one example in particular, that is Dio's *Oration* 7, sometimes known as the *Euboian Oration*, already mentioned briefly in Chapter 1. I choose it for discussion here partly because it shows up that ambivalence in particularly vivid ways, indulging in rhetorical display while also simultaneously introducing very negative images of it. The first half is a first-person narrative about Dio's encounter with a community of country-people during his exile; the second half a denunciation of the evils of city life. The narrative section draws on the *lalia* traditions already mentioned, where the beginning of a speech might be a brief, often allegorical story, to be followed by the main body of advice or argument or praise. Dio, however, vastly expands that narrative element so that it takes up dozens of pages. In that sense the work is a good example of the cross-fertilisation between oratory and novel discussed in Chapter 1: some elements of Dio's pastoral description in fact seem to have influenced Longus' *Daphnis and Chloe*. (For a similarly uncategorisable fictional account of a peculiar rustic encounter one might look at Philostratus' *Heroicus*, which describes a conversation between a Phoenician sailor and a Thracian vinedresser. The vinedresser claims to have direct information about the Trojan War, derived from the semi-divine hero Protesileos, who appears to him regularly, and whose account throws doubt on some of the details of the Homeric version). In the *Euboian Oration* Dio describes being shipwrecked on the shores of Euboia and meeting a huntsman, who offers him hospitality and tells him his life story. He and his family, together with another family, live together in a kind of self-sufficient community far from the city. He tells Dio that he has only visited the city twice himself, and he describes the second of those visits, when he was summoned there to answer the charge of having exploited public land without paying taxes, and was let off only when one of the city dwellers spoke up on his behalf. After a description of the wedding between the son and daughter of the two rustic families Dio then switches quite abruptly, in the second half, into a denunciation of the evils of urban poverty. While this rustic innocence and self-sufficiency is clearly represented as unattainable in practice and even slightly absurd, it is nevertheless clearly intended as an exaggerated emblem of virtues which Dio feels are worth aiming for.

Dio will make another brief appearance in the next chapter, on philosophy, but for now there is space for discussion of just one feature of the narrative and that is the huntsman's description of the speech-making he hears in the city. His innocent outsider's perspective has an estranging effect which leads to a wonderfully fresh and irreverent account of the potential absurdity of oratorical conventions. Our first glimpse comes as he enters the city, describing what he sees with the only language he knows, the language of the countryside, likening the harbour to a lake, and the theatre to a ravine. The speech-making in the Assembly is described in similarly defamiliarising terms:

> To begin with, the crowd was concerned for quite a long time with other matters, and they shouted a lot, sometimes gently and cheerfully, praising certain people, and at other times loudly and angrily. This anger of theirs was a terrible thing: they immediately terrified those people they shouted against, so that some of them ran around imploring them, while others threw off their cloaks through fear. I myself was once nearly knocked over by the shouting as if a wave or thunderbolt had suddenly broken against me (7.24-6).

A reader familiar with traditions of democratic debate will be able to decipher much of what is described here and in the rest of the long description of the trial, but the huntsman is entirely at sea. It is striking, for one thing, that he seems not to have taken in any of the detail of the speeches he hears: the crafted phrases and stirring arguments of these small-time orators make no impression on him, and he hears instead only a confused noise. Striking also is the sense of arbitrary violence of so-called civilisation: the city is a place of fear far more than the countryside, whose relatively benign, idealised features have been described only a little earlier in the huntsman's narrative.

As so often the precise performance context for the text is impossible to reconstruct (indeed in this case, in contrast with some of the examples mentioned above, it is not clear whether the criticisms of the second half are aimed at any particular city), nor can we be sure that it was delivered in precisely this form. Nevertheless the irony of this negative portrayal of oratory is hard to miss in a work which in itself makes such bold use of oratorical resources: the inserted story of the debate sheds a teasingly irreverent light on the context in which Dio and his audience find themselves, distancing Dio from rhetoric even as he indulges in it. In that sense Dio's work – and this oration in particular – is a wonderful example not only of the richness and inventiveness of Imperial Greek oratory, but also of the way in which many of its most gifted practitioners acted out a rather ambivalent relationship with mainstream oratorical and sophistic activity.

Chapter 4

Philosophy

Dio's philosophical pose

Dio's ambivalence towards sophistry is, as we have seen, partly due to the fact that his primary self-identification is as a philosopher. In *Oration* 7 he reminds us of that through the huntsman's queries about his personal appearance:

> 'You seem to me to be one of those city people, not a sailor or someone who works the land; rather you seem to be sick with some great weakness of the body, to judge by your thinness.' I followed him happily, never fearing that I was being plotted against, for I had nothing but a simple cloak. Often at other times too it was my experience in circumstances like this – for I was continually wandering – and indeed in this case too, that poverty is a really holy and inviolable thing, and no one does you any harm ...(7.8-9)

A less naïve speaker than the hunter would recognise the stereotypes of philosophical appearance: physical weakness and shabby clothing which are signs of the philosopher's neglect of worldly passions. The shabby clothes recall Socrates, who was famously unconcerned with his personal appearance. They are also the badge of Cynic philosophy. Cynics rejected worldly vanities even more determinedly than other philosophical schools, and the stereotypical Cynic showed his contempt for convention, and his determination to live according to nature, through a life of wandering and begging. Not all those who expressed Cynic allegiance would have lived such a life: for some, Cynicism was a pose one could adopt or express sympathy with at appropriate moments without going all the way. But Dio himself may well have lived that kind of Cynic lifestyle in the period of his life during which *Oration* 7 is set. Even later in his life he seems to have dressed in this stereotypically Cynic fashion, to judge by the passages in several of his other speeches (e.g. *Oration* 72.2) where he defends himself and others for dressing as philosophers, with long hair and beard. Here then Dio marks out his philosophical status by his appearance, using precisely the signposts of philosophical identity which Lucian mocks so determinedly. It is worth stressing that Dio does not take himself too seriously here. In the passage just quoted there is an ironically self-deprecating joke about the possibility that his philosophical leanings almost literally disqualify him from the idealised life of rustic self-sufficiency he presents to us, because he is not strong enough or robust enough to cope with it. It is almost as though he is aware of the potential for Lucianic mockery of the gap between philosophical appearance and underlying reality (elsewhere he certainly acknowledges that philosophical appearance is not enough to guarantee philosophical character: e.g. 49.11-12).

Philosophical schools

Many other figures similarly laid claim to philosophical identity: Dio is not unusual in this. The picture is complicated, however, by the fact that there were many different focuses of allegiance within the overarching category of philosophy. Here the philosophy of the Roman Empire differs from sophistic culture, which despite the frequency of quarrels over the best way of speaking never had anything resembling these divisions between clearly identifiable philosophical schools. We have already seen a first glimpse of this division of philosophy into different 'schools' or 'sects' in the work of Lucian, who regularly includes a representative of each of the main philosophical groups. In his *Symposium*, for example, each philosopher acts in character, maintaining the superficial markers of his own belief-system while at the same time Lucian advertises the underlying similarity of all of them. The Cynic philosophers have already been mentioned; their philosophy was less a theoretical position and more a choice about how to live. But the other main philosophical schools were based on complex theoretical foundations: the followers of Plato, known sometimes as Academics after the Academy, the philosophical school founded by Plato in Athens; the Aristotelians or Peripatetics; the Stoics (Cynicism had been an important influence on the formation of Stoicism and had some affinities with it – indeed Dio's own primary affiliation as far as his theoretical pronouncements on philosophy are concerned was as a Stoic, and the attack on urban poverty in the second half of *Oration* 7 has been shown to be profoundly influenced by Stoic views); the Epicureans; the Pythagoreans; and finally the Sceptics.

For reasons of space I will make no attempt here at a summary of the philosophical thinking of each of these groups (see Further reading for some starting-points). Summary anyway risks understating the degree of variety in each of these schools. On one level the most important unifying and defining factor for each of these groups was not adherence to an easily summarisable set of doctrines, but rather their loyalty to the thinking of a particular predecessor or set of predecessors from previous centuries. Both Plato and Aristotle came to have revived importance in the Roman period as sources for positive belief-systems. New interpretations of Plato by the third-century philosopher Plotinus led in turn to the growth of 'Neoplatonism', which became the dominant pagan philosophy of the next few centuries, and was influential on some Christian writers. Plotinus' writings, known collectively as the *Enneads*, were published posthumously by his follower Porphyry, who also included a biographical account of Plotinus in the preface, which contributed to his later influence. Stoics and Epicureans looked back to foundational figures who were active in the Hellenistic period: Stoics to the teaching of Zeno and Chrysippus and others; Epicureans to the teaching of Epicurus.

These divisions between different schools had thus been in place well before the period of the Roman Empire, but it nevertheless seems to have been the case that there was increasing philosophical diversity in these centuries, and consequently a new interest in exploring and defining the differences between different areas of philosophical belief. That may be due in part to the break-up of the philosophical teaching institutions of the Epicureans, Stoics and Platonists in late Hellenistic Athens, which ultimately and paradoxically led to a more cosmopolitan presence for each of these schools of thought within wider Mediterranean culture. In the Roman period it becomes increasingly common, too, to read of attacks against rival philosophical approaches as a means of philosophical self-definition.

Nevertheless there is evidence for a great deal of cross-fertilisation between the different schools. We know of some individual figures who drew quite widely from a range of different philosophical approaches without subscribing to any of them exclusively – the medical writer Galen is an obvious example, although he regularly expresses a particular allegiance to Plato. It is in fact surprisingly difficult to find any philo- sophical writer who confines himself strictly to the views of one particular tradition without also using and engaging with the arguments of rival schools: the Epicurean writers are perhaps closest to this kind of exclu- sivism. This is partly because the main philosophical schools were drawn close together through their attention to shared questions and shared areas of exploration, many of which go far beyond the relatively narrow scope of philosophy as we understand it today. Traditionally philosophy had been divided into three separate fields: logic, physics and ethics. Logic dealt with forms of argument, together with linguistics and epistemology (i.e. study of questions about what 'knowledge' is and how it is acquired). Physics dealt with questions about the make-up of the natural world and questions of theology. Ethics covered the question of how one should define proper behaviour, how one should define and achieve happiness and moral progress, how one should manage human emotions; it also covered questions about how civic and household communities ought to be organised. It is the field of ethics which is my main focus in this chapter: physics, particularly in its overlap with what we might in the modern world think of as scientific speculation, will be one of the subjects touched on in Chapter 5. Thus for all the partisanship within different schools, there was also a strong sense of philosophy as an overarching project, a field of study in which the similarities – especially, within ethics, the shared attention to urgent questions about the right way to live – ultimately outweigh the differences. Philosophy, on that model, is separate and independent from all other disciplines; or perhaps better it stands above all other disciplines, guiding them and informing them even as it remains apart from them. That conviction is reflected in the fact that the words philosophy (*philosophia* in Greek), and philosopher (*philosophos*) are used repeatedly within the literature of this period with the implication that they are adequate to describe the action or individual in question, whether or not one chooses in addition to go into the details of affiliation to a particular school.

Cross-fertilisation outside philosophy

For all this sense of the self-sufficiency of philosophy as a discipline, however, it is clear that it had close overlaps with other areas of intellectual activity. There are two areas in particular where those overlaps are apparent. The first is at the level of institutions. Philosophical teaching was viewed as a key element in higher education: young men would often study with philosophers after their basic education in literature with a grammarian; often that higher study of philosophy would come at the same time as education with a rhetor, a teacher of oratory, or sometimes would follow on from that. Philosophy would also often be taught, like rhetoric, through the medium of lectures within the classroom. From Plato onwards, rhetoric had often been represented as antithetical to philosophy, but in practice the two fields were deeply interwoven with each other in institutional terms. We know from Lucian (*Eunuch* 3) and Philostratus (*Lives of the Sophists* 566) that the emperor Marcus Aurelius (on whom more below) assigned at least one public chair or professorship to each of the four main philosophical schools – the Academics, Peripatetics, Stoics and Epicureans, and gave the task of choosing the incumbents to the orator Herodes Atticus, who himself held the chair of rhetoric in Athens. Philosophers were also regularly honoured by their home cities in much the same way as the sophists discussed in Chapter 3, with grants of statues, or with the status of *ateleia*, i.e. freedom from compulsory financial contributions to the running of cities, granted by a succession of emperors.

The second area of overlap – and the main focus of this chapter – is the way in which philosophical writing drew on a wide range of literary forms. When philosophical writers of the Roman Empire write philosophy, they do so in many different ways. Philosophy is not a genre, although there were certain types of writing – especially the Platonic dialogue – which had a strong philosophical heritage. This tendency to range across a variety of different forms is in a sense highly appropriate to the commonly stated ancient doctrine that the true philosopher can do philosophy in any context. It is also appropriate to the principle mentioned above of philosophy as an overarching, guiding discipline which stands above all others. We have already seen something of Dio's generic eclecticism. While he and others like him may not be profound thinkers it would be a great mistake to view him as not engaged in serious philosophy: Imperial philosophy is open to many different ways of engaging with the basic ethical challenge of grappling with problems of the right way to live. Perhaps the most wide-ranging of the philosophical figures of this period is Plutarch, who was not only a profound and subtle thinker on a level far above Dio, but also covered perhaps an even wider generic range. For the moment I want to hold back discussion of Plutarch until Chapters 5 and 7 where we will see how he imbues the genres of miscellanism and biography with philosophical and particularly ethical significance. For the rest of this chapter I survey a number of other Imperial philosophical figures, bearing this question of generic cross-fertilisation particularly in mind.

Maximus of Tyre

My first example is Maximus of Tyre, who was the author of a set of short philosophical speeches dating from the middle of the second century. He is another representative of the rhetorically inflected philosophy which we have seen already for Dio and Favorinus and others: certainly his own occasional allusions to the setting for his speeches hint at a context of quasi-sophistic performance. It is possible, however, that his work reflects above all the context of the classroom outlined above. For example, he several times refers to his addressees as 'young men' (e.g. 1.7 and 1.8), with the implication that his speeches between them offer an outline philosophical education. Much of his work concentrates on making philosophy easy and accessible, and it may be that he particularly has in mind an audience who are not interested in high-level philosophical engagement. His speeches have a strong literary texture, quoting regularly in particular from Homer, and a tendency to avoid philosophical jargon, both of which must have increased their appeal to non-specialists. He has a particularly strong interest in Plato, although he does not identify himself at any point as a Platonist, preferring instead to see philosophy as a pursuit which stands above partisan divisions, and which is again all the more accessible for that. The titles of his speeches give some indication of the themes they cover: 'What is the aim of philosophy?' (*Oration* 2); 'How might one ready oneself for dealings with a friend?' (*Oration* 4); 'Whether images should be set up in honour of the gods' (*Oration* 6); 'Whether one ought to repay wrong with wrong' (*Oration* 12). These are all standard concerns of ancient ethics. Other speeches, however, come closer to the character of sophistic rhetoric. In several cases, for example, Maximus gives opposite answers to the same question in successive speeches: for example 'Whether there exists one Good greater than another; that there does not' (*Oration* 33); 'Whether there exists one Good greater than another; that there does' (*Oration* 34). And in several cases we see ingenuity which would not be out of place in a sophistic speech, for example in *Oration* 26, which argues that Homer is the first and greatest of philosophers.

Epictetus

More clearly linked with classroom education are the writings of Epictetus, one of the most distinctive and engaging voices of Imperial-period philosophy. The texts which survive are effectively records of lectures delivered to his pupils, although here again it is difficult to be sure of how the words on paper relate to what was actually delivered, since they are recorded in the *Discourses* by his pupil Arrian (discussed further in Chapter 6), who sets out to preserve the words of his master in much the same way as Plato or Xenophon preserved the teaching of Socrates. Epictetus was an emancipated slave, and it is tempting to feel that that experience feeds into his work, with its stress on the importance of self-sufficiency and of maintaining one's equilibrium in the face of whatever external misfortunes life brings. His message is influenced in particular by Stoic sympathies, although once again he draws widely from the full range of philosophical resources. As for Maximus, although more convincingly, one might feel, Epictetus' priority is to communicate the urgency of engaging with philosophy as a non-partisan pursuit of truth and knowledge about the best way to live. His philosophical persona is wonderfully passionate and persuasive, full of vivid images and metaphors and direct appeals which seem to speak to each reader or listener individually. His stress on the importance of self-attention and the use of good judgement in response to circumstance are not unusual in the philosophy of this period, but are rarely articulated quite so memorably anywhere else. Above all, Epictetus' work is a powerful demonstration of why philosophy mattered to so many of the inhabitants of the Roman Empire.

I quote here, just to give one example, one of the shorter chapters of the work, addressed 'To those who wish to be admired' (*Discourses* 1.21):

> Whenever someone has the status he deserves in life, he does not long for anything beyond that. 'What is it, man, that you wish to happen to you?' 'I am satisfied if my desires and disinclinations are in accord with nature, if my impulses and my desires to refrain from action are in accord with my own nature, along with my aims and my designs and my assent.' 'Why then do you walk around looking as though you've swallowed a poker?' 'My desire was that those who meet me should admire, and those who follow behind me should cry out, "What a great philosopher!"' 'Who are these people you want to be admired by? Aren't they precisely the people you usually describe as mad? What then? Do you want to be admired by people who are mad?'

Some parts of this extract use the jargon of Stoic philosophy – especially the pompous imagined response to Epictetus' initial question. But that engagement with complex philosophical ideals is counterbalanced by the simplicity and vividness of Epictetus' language. The imagined dialogue, and the second-person address to an imagined interlocutor, which we as readers can hardly fail to feel is addressed to us, are entirely typical of Epictetus' style. Moreover, Epictetus, like Dio and like Lucian, is very much aware of the problem of those who do philosophy badly, who value outward appearance and outward renown at the expense of true, underlying philosophical commitment.

Marcus Aurelius

Perhaps Epictetus' most famous reader was Marcus Aurelius. One of the remarkable things about Marcus Aurelius is simply the fact that he was emperor of Rome: his devotion to philosophy illustrates the degree to which philosophy was embedded within elite culture, even within the Roman culture of the Latin-speaking west. Rome's engagement with Greek philosophy had begun many centuries before, with particularly important landmarks in the literature of the late Republic, especially in the writing of Cicero and Lucretius. Examples of self-control and virtue had always been viewed as positive signs for an emperor's government of the empire, as we can see through even a quick glance at the work of the Latin biographer of the emperors, Suetonius. Nevertheless, it is still extraordinary to see the emperor of Rome writing philosophy in Greek, not least because philosophy had at times, even in the century before Marcus Aurelius was writing and ruling, been viewed as a pursuit to be treated with caution by the Roman elite. The Roman historian Tacitus, writing the biography of his father-in-law, the distinguished politician and general Agricola, expresses his approval of the fact that Agricola's early enthusiasm for philosophy was tempered (*Agricola* 4.3). Philosophers had even at times been viewed as politically subversive figures, and had been banished (among them Epictetus' famous teacher, the Stoic philosopher Musonius) from the city of Rome by several different emperors. But the other remarkable thing about Marcus Aurelius' writing, and the thing which is my main interest here, is simply the form of it. His writings, in Greek, are collectively known as the *Meditations*. They take the form of short and intense moralising reflections on the best way to live. In that sense they act out Epictetus' call to painstaking self-attention. And in some ways they form a parallel to the bodily self-attention, in similar first-person diary form, of Aelius Aristides' *Sacred Tales*. By the standards of modern diary writing or autobiography they are strikingly – and even at first sight disappointingly – impersonal, but they nevertheless form an intriguing landmark within this period's new fascination with the possibilities of first-person speech, which we have glimpsed already in Chapters 1 and 2 for Lucian and the novel. All these works between them prepare the way for the development of new Christian uses of the confessional first-person voice, most famously in St Augustine's *Confessions*, written in the late fourth century, which divert the traditions of philosophical self-attention to new uses.

Diogenes of Oenoanda

My fourth and final example is in a sense the most extraordinary of all these examples of philosophical self-projection, and that is the work of the Epicurean Diogenes of Oenoanda. Like the writings of Marcus Aurelius, this text demonstrates the potential for the private life of philosophy to be entwined with the world of politics, and yet in other ways it could not be more different. Where Marcus Aurelius seems often to be addressing himself, conjuring up an image of the most private of meditations, Diogenes' text addresses the world in the most public way imaginable, through being inscribed on stone in the middle of his native city of Oenoanda in Lycia, what is now southern Turkey, around 200 CE. The text itself seems to have been enormous – perhaps as many as 120 columns of writing, covering 40 metres of wall; and the excavation and piecing together of the remaining fragments was a considerable achievement of scholarly detective work. It was not unusual for texts to be inscribed in public in the ancient world. Every city of the Roman Empire would have been crammed with inscriptions recording the benefactions of wealthy members of the city, or the city's decrees or rulings of the emperor. But Diogenes' manipulation of that resource for philosophical purposes is as far we know unique, and all the more remarkable for the Epicurean tradition of avoiding engagement with politics. His benefaction to the city of Oenoanda, it implies, is the Epicurean wisdom which the stones offer to those who read them: he takes over the space of political inscription, claiming it for philosophy.

Here too, also remarkable given the impersonal style of most other ancient inscriptions, with their formal recording of civic business, we find a very engaging and distinctive personal voice. Once again, the urgency of Diogenes' message comes across powerfully. Diogenes speaks, for example, about his own illness and approaching death in ways which bring out vividly the power of the Epicurean principle that death is not to be feared:

> And so, having laid out the second reason for writing this, I will now go on to explain my mission, and to describe what it is like and what character it has. For standing already in the sunset of my life, because of old age, and being almost on the point of departing from my life, I wanted, by composing a cheerful song to celebrate the fullness of pleasure, to give help to all discriminating people, in order that I should not be snatched away before I achieve this. (fragment 3)

And later:

> I follow you when you make these claims about death, and you have persuaded me to laugh at it; for I am not afraid on account of the Tityoses and the Tantaloses, who some people say are in Hades, nor

do I shudder when I think about the putrefaction of the body, believing that there is no suffering for us, when the soul has disappeared, nor anything else. (fragment 73)

The inscriptional form turns out to be curiously well suited to the needs of Epicurean discourse, which tends to rely heavily on short and memorable phrases designed to stick in the mind of the listener: a bystander browsing through the text might be able to take away important precepts and principles even from a very cursory perusal.

Christian uses of Greek philosophy

Much of the Greek philosophy of the Roman Empire is considerably more technical, and considerably more difficult, than the examples I have given here, and a fuller account would need to do more to get to grips with the difficult interpretative challenges of that work. My main aim here has been not only to demonstrate something of the generic range and inventiveness of Imperial philosophy, in keeping with the wider themes of this book, but also to suggest how compelling and how accessible some of the voices of ancient philosophy can be, in their attempts to grapple with urgent problems which still in many ways matter to us, problems about how to live our lives.

In the final section of this chapter I want to turn briefly to Christian uses of Greek philosophical traditions. Christian writing is still all too often neglected in classical scholarship on the Greek literature of the Roman Empire. The relevance of Lucianic satire and sophistic rhetoric to Christian literature are admittedly relatively marginal (although recent scholarship has begun to reveal the way in which some early Christian texts – for example the New Testament writings of Paul – engage with and sometimes reject the techniques of Greco-Roman oratory). For this chapter on philosophy, however, and for several of the chapters which follow, Christian culture cannot be so easily ignored. We have seen already how ancient philosophy tended to cover many of the concerns which we would today categorise as religious or theological issues, so in that sense it should be no surprise that many early Christian authors saw it as an important resource for interrogating and forming new Christian ideas about the make-up of the world and about the right way to live. Latching on to philosophical traditions was part of a much wider strategy of advertising their compatibility with Greco-Roman culture, just one of many ways in which early Christian authors attempted to persuade their listeners of the legitimacy of the Christian message. It was also a technique which many Jewish writers had adopted in previous centuries. Several of the Christian apologists (the word *apologia* in Greek means 'defence' and refers in this context to works which attempt to reverse the criticisms made of Christianity by its pagan accusers) address their works to the philosopher-emperor Marcus Aurelius, a sign of the way in which they are attempting to tap into the respectable position which philosophy had increasingly come to attain within Greco-Roman elite culture.

What form did this rewriting of Greek philosophy take? To take just one example, Christian belief in monotheism, which was one of the flashpoints in pagan anger against Christian communities, who refused to participate in sacrificial rituals for the many pagan deities, was regularly justified by the apologists through reference to claims about monotheism to be found within Greco-Roman philosophy, for example within middle Platonic thought, which was itself influenced by Stoic and Peripatetic tradition. The concept of the Divine Logos or 'Word' as the revealer of divine truth is also routinely linked by Christian writers with Greek philosophical ideas. Justin Martyr, for example, speaks as follows:

> Philosophy is in reality the greatest and most precious possession. It leads us to God, and it alone unites us, and those who have turned their minds to philosophy are truly holy. (*Dialogue with Trypho* 2.1)

Here the standard philosophical imagery of progress towards virtue is redirected to a specifically Christian context. Justin acknowledges the truth of Greek philosophy, although he also stresses that the Greco-Roman philosophers had only partial access to the divine Logos – it is only through faith in Christ that one can gain access to it in full. Many other Christian apologists are less complimentary than Justin about pagan philosophy – notably the Latin writer Tertullian, and the Greek Tatian – but even these do follow Justin's lead at least to the extent of proclaiming Christianity as the true philosophy, reclaiming the prestigious label of philosophy for themselves. Nor does early Christian culture confine itself to abstract theological borrowings from Greek philosophy. For instance, Christian teachings on chastity themselves draw on Greco-Roman philosophical ideas. And the representation of the Christian holy men in the Apocryphal Acts, discussed briefly above in Chapter 1, often draws on the imagery of the philosopher.

The form of Christian apology also often borrows from the philosophical writings of the pre-Christian past. For instance, a number of Christian writers manipulate the traditions of philosophical protreptic – the kind of writing which attempts to convert its readers to philosophical commitment. Clement of Alexandria's *Protrepticus*, to take just one example, follows a standard tripartite protreptic structure: rejection of rival philosophies, followed by positive recommendation of the belief system to be followed, closing with a more personal appeal to the reader for conversion. Other apologists exploit the Platonic dialogue form: the most engaging example of all is probably Justin Martyr. In one of the earliest works of Christian apologetics, for example, the *Dialogue with Trypho* (from which I quoted above) he describes a conversation with a Jewish interlocutor in which he explains and justifies his conversion to Christianity, representing that move as a conversion to philosophy, marked by his wearing of philosophical dress. The inventiveness, theological sophistication and argumentative brilliance of Imperial Greek philosophy thus find a powerful new home in early Christian literature. In some ways the dogmatic character of Christian apology might seem far removed from the commitment to open-ended debate which marks the work of Plato and many of his successors, but it is nevertheless a natural extension of the urgency which characterises so much of the ethical discussion of the Roman Empire, and which we have glimpsed in the passionate voices of Epictetus and Diogenes of Oenoanda and others.

Chapter 5
Science and Miscellanism

The prestige of compilation

We have seen already that some of what we would categorise today as 'science' was viewed in the ancient world as part of the province of philosophy. There are vast numbers of scientific texts surviving from the Imperial period, many of which make strong claims for their own philosophical significance. However, I have kept this material separate from Chapter 4 in order to suggest that there is much to be gained from viewing ancient scientific writing within the wider context of ancient knowledge compilation. The aim of accumulating vast amounts of information was widespread within the literature of this period, in both Latin and Greek. Compilation is not a genre – rather a shared mode of writing across many disciplines. Some of the texts we will look at in this chapter do cover traditionally philosophical questions of natural science; others, however, accumulated knowledge for the more pragmatic purposes of teaching their readers mastery of particular technical disciplines; others again, particularly miscellanies, with their deliberately mixed collections of curious material, focus more on entertainment. This vast enterprise of knowledge compilation looked back to the Hellenistic world, for example to the scholarship of third-century BCE Alexandria, where polymathic scholars and poets flocked to the court of the Ptolemies, the rulers of Egypt; and even further back to the work of Aristotle, with its systematising ambition to cover so many different fields of human knowledge. But it also seems to be the case that compilation took on a new scale and a new importance in the Imperial period. To take just one example, the fact that many of the sophistic and philosophical figures we have looked at in previous chapters themselves wrote works of compilation gives some idea of its central place within the literary culture of the second century: Polemo, for example, wrote a long treatise on physiognomics – the art of deciphering character from physical appearance; Favorinus and Herodes Atticus both wrote works of miscellany.

Clearly compilatory styles of writing were much more prestigious than they are today. How do we explain that fact? What was the attraction of these works? (both for their original readers and indeed for the readers of the Renaissance, where they were widely revered and imitated). Our own images of what authorship involves and of what kinds of authorial endeavour are to be valued are themselves a product of cultural and historical forces, even if that is not obvious to us. Other times and places have not always shared our own obsession with originality, which is in part an inheritance of eighteenth-century Romantic fascination with the ideal of inspired artistic creation. Within the Greek (and indeed Latin) literature of the Roman Empire, originality mattered less. Reverence for the literature of the past was a key part of this society's commitment to tradition. The image of the author as a compiler, showing his readers a way through the vast territory of already discovered knowledge, and through the virtual library made up of earlier writings, was accordingly highly valued. That is apparent immediately from the prevalence of doxographical styles of composition, which was developed first of all within writing on the history of philosophy, but which also influenced other areas of scientific and miscellanistic discussion: doxography is the technique of laying out in turn the views of a number of different predecessors on the particular question under discussion. Moreover, these styles of composition often had the potential to comment on the social and political world around them, despite the initial impression of them as dry, abstract and inaccessible works. In many cases, for example, we come to see on closer inspection that their very diverse collections of material are in fact unified by a consistent moralising perspective. Some scholars have even viewed the literary enterprise of knowledge compilation as parallel to, necessary for or even in rivalry with the accumulation of territory and expertise on which the Roman Empire was founded – although one needs to be careful about over-generalising on that issue, since different texts represent the relations between knowledge and the political world differently, and the link is more obvious for some than for others (Pliny the Elder's encyclopaedic Latin work, the *Natural History*, discussed further below, is one particularly good example).

Before going any further, it may be helpful simply to list some of the areas to which these compilatory techniques were central. The genre of miscellanistic writing I have mentioned already, and also the body of philosophical writing on the workings of the natural world. The doxographical techniques discussed above were also standardly used in works of ethical philosophy. In addition, however, we have surviving compilatory manuals on a vast range of other subjects, including (to name only the most obvious) the following: medicine (in its many different branches), farming, land surveying, architecture, rhetoric, grammar,

mathematics, music, lexicography, generalship, law, dream interpretation, hunting, astrology, physiognomics and athletic training. In addition
this compilatory, encyclopaedic obsession spreads into the material discussed in other chapters – geography, history, biography, even poetry,
where anthologisation was common. The compilatory obsession even
leaves its mark on the Greek novels, as we shall see briefly towards the
end of the chapter.

Galen: medicine and philosophy

Within that list of disciplines it is sometimes hard to see exactly where
philosophy ends and technical manual-writing begins, partly because it
was commonplace to make ingenious claims for the philosophical character of one's own writing even when the philosophical connection was
fairly tenuous. For example the first-century scientific author Heron of
Alexandria, in his treatise on *The Construction of Artillery*, ingeniously
claims that his writing will help to achieve *ataraxia* ('peace of mind'),
which is the word used for the traditional goal of Epicurean philosophy:
military security is of course not quite what Epicurus had in mind. In other
cases, however, the philosophical commitments of technical authors are
more deeply held. Here I want to focus on one example, and that is the
work of the medical writer Galen, whose output represents one of the most
ambitious of all projects of knowledge compilation surviving from the
ancient world, and who was entirely serious in his claims for medicine as
a philosophical discipline. His treatise *The Best Doctor is also a Philosopher* argues that position at length. His work also assumes that understanding of medicine should be inextricably tied up with understanding
of the divine intelligence which has ordered creation, and which has
constructed the human body so wonderfully, crafting each part with a
particular goal in mind. The volume of his work is astonishing. Much of
it does not survive, but what does fills up 22 very large volumes in the
standard nineteenth-century edition (not including those works which
survive only in Arabic). The intellectual range of his writing is also
extraordinary. He ranges across all branches of the field of medicine
as it was defined within the ancient world, writing particularly exten-
sively on diet and botany and on anatomy and the physiology of the
human body. His work also includes a number of treatises which seek
to define and exalt the art of medicine over rival disciplines. In addition
he wrote commentaries on the works of those he saw as his greatest
predecessors: Plato and the medical writings generally ascribed (by
Galen and others) to the fifth-century BCE medic Hippocrates. Some of

his writing even strays far beyond the territory which we would see as relevant to medicine: for example he seems to have written some treatises on the choices of vocabulary made by the classical Athenian comic poets. This is the kind of polymathy, bridging right across modern disciplinary boundaries, which is common in ancient literature, even if few exercised it quite so comprehensively as Galen. The extent of his writing, built up across a whole lifetime, means that Galen faces a great challenge to impose order even on his own output, let alone on the knowledge of his predecessors: two of his works, *On My Own Books* and *On the Order of My Own Books*, offer lengthy lists and categorisations of his own works.

One of the most striking features of Galen's authorial voice is the stridency and self-confidence of his own professional self-projection, which goes far beyond the more cautious, self-effacing authorial presence we find in much other compilatory literature, and at times even seems to have more in common with the arrogance of the sophists as Philostratus describes them. Some of his work is very technical and difficult, presumably written up from lecture notes. But at other times, when Galen pulls out all the stops, his writing can be compelling: it is hard to think of another equally competitive author anywhere in ancient literature, and his passionate denunciation of his rivals is hard to forget once read. Here Galen's independent-mindedness is important: he insists throughout his work on the importance of proof and correct argumentation (indeed his works on logic are among the most sophisticated to survive from the ancient world). He made important advances in medical science which were effectively the foundation of both Islamic and western European medicine through the medieval period and the Renaissance and beyond. He has nothing but contempt for those who follow like sheep in the tracks of received opinion without interrogating it for themselves. Even Galen, however, makes use of the doxographical techniques of so many of his contemporaries: he is acutely aware of what his various predecessors have argued for on any particular issue, and he stresses his devotion to Plato and Hippocrates repeatedly, albeit in a way which sometimes ingeniously distorts the contents of their work, reinventing them in his own image.

One of the other great attractions of Galen's work, finally, is for the social historian of ancient science. They are a great treasure-trove of information about the social and intellectual context of ancient medicine: Galen's regular mentions of his rivals and students and clients helps to build up a picture of the kinds of communities and relationships which grew up around medical activity. This was a world without formal medical qualifications, where the doctor was engaged in a constant struggle to prove himself. Some of the most memorable of Galen's works describe public debate against rival physicians. In one scene, for example, he dissects an elephant in order to prove to his doubting peers that elephants have bones (actually pieces of hardened cartilage) in their hearts. And for the most successful of doctors the rewards were great: Galen was effectively official physician to the imperial family, appointed as such by the philosopher-emperor Marcus Aurelius. The confidence of his authorial voice at least in that sense seems to have been entirely justified.

Plutarch: miscellanism and philosophy

What Galen's work – and most of the other technical fields listed above – have in common is that they at least purport to convey one particular, clearly bounded area of knowledge or expertise. Miscellanism – to which I now turn – is rather different. It is a standard gesture in the preface to miscellanistic works to claim that one is writing primarily to entertain; also that one has arranged one's material at random. However, it would be wrong to see even miscellanism as an entirely frivolous genre. These texts must for some readers have had a practical purpose in making accessible material which could be used in conversation to project an impression of cultured elite identity. The volume of writing available from the previous centuries of Greek literary endeavour was daunting, far too much for most ordinary mortals to gain mastery over, and miscellanies could act as helpful short-cuts. In some cases, too, we see moralising aims underlying an apparently disparate collection of material. Once again, we know at least enough to be sure that the genre of miscellanistic writing was well populated. For example the Latin miscellanist Aulus Gellius, discussed further briefly below, lists thirty rival titles in the preface to his own work the *Attic Nights*.

One particularly influential text in the history of miscellanistic writing was Plutarch's *Sympotic Questions*. The work is a record, so Plutarch claims, of learned conversations between himself and his friends at drinking parties from many decades of his life, written up, presumably, in the early years of the second century. Each conversation (95 of them in all, over nine books) is dedicated to discussion of one or more questions, with different speakers contributing in turn. The topics of discussion range from questions specifically associated with Greek customs of eating and drinking, through to questions of science and literature and local history. The topics of Book 4, for example, are as follows: 'Whether a variety of food is more easily digested than a single kind'; 'Why truffles seem to be brought into being by thunder, and why people think that people who are sleeping cannot be struck by thunderbolts'; 'Why it is that people invite the most guests to dinner at weddings'; 'Whether the sea is richer in delicacies than the land'; 'Whether the Jews abstain from pork because of respect for or disgust at the pig'; 'Who the god of the Jews is'; 'Why days named after the planets are arranged not in the same order as the planetary position, but in reverse order; also on the position of the sun'; 'Why people wear seal rings most of all on the finger next to the middle finger'; 'Whether it is necessary to wear images of the gods or of wise men on seal rings'; 'Why women do not eat the heart of lettuces'. The variety of topics is absolutely typical of miscellanistic writing, as is the doxographical method, whereby the speakers regularly cite from earlier authors in their attempts to answer the questions under discussion. That said, it is important to be clear about the fact that this work stands out from the broader miscellanistic tradition through being descended from the symposium works of Plato and Xenophon (the tradition which is satirised by Lucian in his *Symposium* and *On Salaried Posts*, as we have seen already in Chapter 2). A number of other miscellanistic works in this genre survive from the same period, most notably the *Sophists at Dinner* of Athenaeus, which records conversations between a set of implausibly learned intellectuals quoting at enormous length from classical and Hellenistic Greek writing about food and drink. In Plutarch's work, too, a high proportion of the conversation is on topics connected with eating and drinking, although he (unlike Athenaeus) mixes that material with other topics of scientific and cultural enquiry.

I have suggested that miscellany, for all its claims about the importance of entertainment, often has a didactic agenda of sorts beneath the surface. That is true for Plutarch perhaps more so than for any other ancient miscellanist. For one thing we should note the importance of the specific social context of these conversations. The vividly described scene-setting at the beginning of each chapter conjures up a fascinating image of a cosmopolitan elite society, made up of dinner-party guests from many different Greek cities, unified by a common love of the Greek cultural and literary heritage. Some chapters are set in Plutarch's home town of Chaironeia (Plutarch maintained a commitment to local politics throughout his life), some in other cities, many at festival occasions. By stressing the importance of specific social occasions, Plutarch goes beyond the technique of simply stringing facts together, as a resource for the reader's own conversation; instead he shows us knowledge in action. He shows us, for example, young men attending the symposia and learning from their elders about the best ways to solve problems and to display their erudition. The implication is that we as readers can learn in similar fashion from the conversations he shows us.

It is crucial, too, to view the *Sympotic Questions* within the context of Plutarch's wider body of work. Like Galen, Plutarch's whole life was devoted to philosophy, and to the accumulation of knowledge, envisaged as a philosophical project. His writing may not quite match the bulk of Galen's, but if anything it goes beyond Galen's work in its intellectual range. Plutarch is one of the most subtle and compelling and influential of all ancient Greek prose authors, although his work is not always easy to read. His massive project of biographical writing, the *Lives*, we shall see more of in Chapter 7. Even biography, for Plutarch, was ultimately a philosophical, moralising activity. More relevant for this chapter is the rest of his work, known collectively by its Latin title as the *Moralia* (the Greek word is *Ethika* – meaning literally 'Ethical things'). The *Sympotic Questions* is just one of dozens of works in that extraordinarily diverse corpus, including dialogues (some of them historical, set in the distant Greek past), works of advice on politics, health, marriage, friendship and education (along with many other moralising subjects), collections of sayings from famous historical figures, other works on questions of natural science, discussion of the teachings of a range of different philosophical schools (Plutarch himself is primarily a Platonist), quasi-anthropological discussion of the origins of Greek and Roman customs – all of these texts unified by Plutarch's abiding interest in recurring ethical questions about how life ought to be lived. In the context of that wider body of work, accumulated over Plutarch's whole life, the miscellanism of the *Sympotic Questions*, for all its light-heartedness, comes to look like part of a rather more serious project than initially appears to be the case. It is a work which teaches us, like so many of Plutarch's other works, how we can take curiosity as a starting-point for philosophy, and how we can use the enormous literary and philosophical heritage of the Greek past as a springboard for independent thinking.

Christian miscellanism: Clement of Alexandria

Some of the more classicising authors of early Christian literature made use of miscellanistic conventions for new Christian purposes. One of the earliest examples is Clement of Alexandria, whom we have met briefly already, and who wrote his *Stromateis* ('Patchwork') probably in the first years of the third century. For Clement, too, miscellanism is a serious business. The work shares with Greco-Roman miscellanism the initial appearance of disjointedness, moving between a wide range of subjects.

But when we step back from the details it becomes clear that the work as a whole is in fact tightly focused on the aim of providing a starting-point for 'gnostic' theology, laying out the moral personality of the ideal gnostic, whose training will allow him to reach a spiritual understanding of the revelations laid out in the Scriptures. In that sense Clement's interest in combining references to Greco-Roman literature with biblical quotation and polemical discussion of the views of other recent and contemporary Christian thinkers is not just a sign of stereotypical miscellanistic indiscriminacy, but also an index of his desire to make Christian teaching compatible with Greco-Roman philosophical insights.

Aelian

In most other cases, however, the moralising quality of miscellanism is more superficial than it is for Clement or Plutarch. One good example here is the sophist Aelian, who was roughly contemporary with Clement. He is known mainly for two works: the *Historical Miscellany* and *On the Characteristics of Animals*. Both are highly entertaining works to dip into. Neither of them comes even close to matching the philosophical depth of Plutarch's miscellanism, despite the fact that they sometimes cover similar ground in looking at questions of natural science or local history – although the preface to *On the Characteristics of Animals* hints in passing at a serious purpose in provoking reflection on the relation between human nature and the natural world: 'the fact that irrational animals should by nature have some share of virtue, and should have many of mankind's excellences and amazing qualities assigned to them also, this is an amazing thing'. Some of the chapters which follow do indeed fit in with that broad theme. Moreover, Aelian shows signs of a commitment to Stoic moralising – although not a particularly complex version of Stoic moralising – in the assumptions he makes about divine providence, and in his suggestion that seeing human vices and virtues in animals can teach us the virtues of reason and self-control.

People say that the jackal is the most friendly animal to humans. Whenever it happens to come across a human, it moves out of the way, as if through respect; but when it sees a human being harmed by some other animal, under those circumstances it protects him. (1.7)

The octopus banquets first on one food and then on another, for it is both a prodigious eater and exceptionally cunning in making plots, the reason being that it is the most omnivorous of all sea creatures. Proof of this is the fact that if it fails to catch any food it takes a bite from its own tentacles, and filling its stomach like this it makes amends for its lack of prey. Later what is missing grows back, Nature seeming to provide this ready meal in times of famine. (1.27)

There is nothing, however, which even comes close to Plutarch's elaborate didactic framing, and his insistence on thinking independently beyond the material one inherits from the classical tradition.

When Aelian claims in his preface that his main aim is to make accessible the researches of others, we should probably take him more at face value than in Plutarch's case – although that does not mean that his work would necessarily have had less appeal for being derivative. This is a perfect illustration of the point I made towards the beginning of the chapter that the image of author as consolidator of past traditions could be an enormously prestigious one, as could the ideal of delving into the virtual world of the Greek library to dig out things which are surprising and unexpected. Moreover, Aelian himself was very far being just an obscure antiquarian: he was a sophist, and praised as such by Philostratus (*Lives of the Sophists* 624-5), who paints him as a highly respected figure.

Latin compilatory writing and Greek tradition

Latin compilatory writing is also relevant here, since it often draws heavily on Greek traditions, and since it can reveal to us a great deal about the literary culture of the Roman Empire, where Romans (many of whom were bilingual in Greek and Latin) and members of the Greek elites from the east of the empire, associated with each other closely. Plutarch shows a number of Roman guests at his drinking parties contributing to conversation and displaying their command over Greek methods of argumentation and their knowledge of Greek philosophical writing. Aelian was himself a Roman, and is said to have boasted that he had never left the shores of Italy: like Favorinus, he is a wonderful example of how Greek culture becomes accessible in this period to outsiders. Another good example here is Aulus Gellius, whose *Attic Nights* is one of the most famous and influential of ancient miscellanies. He spent a long period in Athens, and was clearly immersed in Greek literature and culture. He describes encounters with a wide range of important intellectual contemporaries, including the philosophers and grammarians and rhetors who were his teachers. He was devoted in particular to Favorinus, and gives many examples of occasions when Favorinus displayed his erudition; he also describes Herodes Atticus on a number of occasions (for example,

Attic Nights 1.2 gives a wonderfully vivid description of a visit to Herodes' villa where Herodes chastises a pompous young dinner guest for his ignorance). Gellius is thus saturated in Greek literary culture. At the same time, however, he works hard to Romanise the Greek miscellanising traditions he follows: his attention to obscure grammatical and antiquarian questions concerning the Latin language and Latin literature make his Roman perspective hard to miss.

The other Roman author who is important here is the elder Pliny, whose *Natural History* was composed in the late first century CE. He has much in common with the miscellanistic authors so far discussed, but his work is more usually referred to as an encyclopaedia. There is no clear dividing line between miscellany and encyclopaedia, and it is probably best to view both of these as a modes of writing rather than clearly delineated genres. Nevertheless 'encyclopaedic' writers tend to be distinguished by claims they make about a kind of totalising ambition for their work, a desire to include the whole substance of human knowledge. Pliny regularly draws our attention to the vast number of previous works he has read in constructing his *Natural History*. Many of these works are Greek; in addition he refers to the Greek ideal of *enkyklios paideia* (literally 'encircling education', and the origin of the modern word 'encyclopaedia'), the set of key subjects which between them were thought to give a student a broad general education. Pliny constructs a monumental, Roman version of *enkyklios paideia* through his work. In that sense the *Natural History* is another good illustration of the degree to which Greek literary culture embeds itself in Roman elite consciousness.

Paradoxography and the ancient novel

One other strand of compilatory writing needs to be mentioned finally, and that is the body of literature often known as paradoxography – the recording of strange facts. Many of the authors already mentioned at times come close to being included in this category: Aelian, for example, with his peculiar facts about animal behaviour. Paradoxography also often plays a role within ethnography and geography which will be the subject of the chapter following. But there are a number of writers who present paradoxographical material in more undiluted form. The Greek writer Phlegon, for example, who seems to have been a freed slave of the emperor Hadrian, wrote a work *On Marvels*, which has survived in part, containing (among other things) ghost stories, examples of sex-changers and hermaphrodites, stories about finds of giant bones, monstrous and multiple births, and discoveries of live centaurs.

However, my reason for mentioning it here is because of the way in which paradoxography – and indeed the wider culture of miscellanism and scientific speculation – makes its mark on the Greek novels. Many of them contain passages which are clearly meant to appeal to precisely the kinds of audience who may have taken pleasure in the work of Aelian or perhaps even Plutarch's more elevated and sophisticated versions of the same trends. Achilles Tatius' character Menelaos at one point describes an elephant:

> The jaw of the elephant is like the head of an ox; looking at it you would say that the mouth itself has two horns growing out of it, but in fact this is the curved tooth of the elephant … Once I saw a strange sight: a Greek man inserted his head into the middle of the animal's head, and the elephant kept its mouth open, and breathed around the man as he stayed inside. I was amazed, both at the man, for his audacity and at the elephant, for his tolerance. The man said that he had in fact given a fee to the animal because its exhaled breath is almost indistinguishable from Indian spices and is a remedy for a sore head. (4.4)

This description has thematic significance for the action around it – most importantly because the heroine Leukippe is herself the object of male looking in the same way as the wild animals who are on display at this point (as Helen Morales has shown – see Further reading): 'We kept our eyes on the beast' – in this case a captured hippopotamus, discussion of which then leads into the digression on elephants – 'but the general was eyeing Leukippe, and suddenly he was trapped' (4.3) (i.e. in love with her). Here Leukippe is herself described in quite dehumanised, male-cen- tred terms, as a wild creature, to be captured and tamed. The general too risks being associated with animalistic identity himself, if we equate his metaphorical capture with the capture of the hippopotamus; alternatively we might see him as equivalent here to a human captured by a wild beast and in danger. Here, then, we are seeing miscellanistic knowledge in action: this passage, like many others in the novels, is typical of the way in which peculiar facts could be picked out and redeployed in new contexts, used in conversa- tion or in story-telling. More generally speaking, we are seeing in this passage signs of the enormously wide appeal of scientific speculation, paradoxogra- phy, and factual compilation, and its diffusion into almost every corner of the Greek literature of the Imperial period.

Chapter 6

History and Geography

Pre-Roman past and Roman present

We have already seen something of the fascination the past holds for the Greek culture of the Roman period. With that in mind, it is no surprise to see that many Imperial-period Greek historians look back beyond the period of Roman rule to the classical and Hellenistic worlds. The *Anabasis* of Arrian, his account of the expeditions of Alexander, is a case in point: he was himself a powerful politician in Rome, and an archetypal example of the integration of the Greek elites into Roman politics, and yet chose to write above all of the pre-Roman world, glorifying the conquests of Alexander, the only Greek figure whose empire rivalled that of the Romans. He also used, as a role-model for his own writing, the classical Athenian soldier-author Xenophon (Arrian's editing and publication of the works of Epictetus, already discussed in Chapter 4, follows the precedent of Xenophon's writing about Socrates).

However, the tendency to ignore or marginalise Rome on closer inspection has many exceptions. As far back as the work of Polybius in the second century BCE the relations between Greece and Rome had been a topic of particular fascination for Greek historians (Polybius himself, as a prominent Greek politician held hostage in Rome, was writing in part from his own experiences), as had the challenge of deciphering Roman culture for a Greek audience. That interest in the origins of Rome's empire is apparent similarly in the work of Appian, in the first half of the second century CE, who charts the Roman conquest in a range of different regions in turn. Plutarch's historical biographies, which we will look at in the next chapter, pair Greek and Roman subjects, measuring them up against each other for their virtues and vices (although most of his subjects date from many centuries before the time of writing). Dionysius of Halicarnassus, writing soon after Augustus came to power, praises Rome in his *Roman Antiquities*, and also argues at length that Rome is a Greek city – an extreme manifestation of the Polybian project of making Rome familiar and understandable for Greek readers. Some Greek historians even look closer to their own time. Cassius Dio, for example, covers a vast period from the foundation of the city of Rome up to the present day (229 CE). Herodian's work has a much less ambitious chronological scope, but he too charts recent Roman history down to his own day, covering the period 180-238 CE. The Jewish writer Josephus traces the development of Jewish culture from its earliest days, but also writes on the very recent history of conflict between Rome and the Jews in the first century CE, drawing in part, like Polybius, on his own experiences. Christian writers in turn appropriate these historiographical traditions. Most influential was Eusebius' *Ecclesiastical History*, written in the first decades of the fourth century, which set out to show the workings of God's plan through the whole of human history by charting the growth of the church from the time of Jesus up to the emperor Constantine's christianisation of the empire in the present.

Historical geography/geographical history

Other surveys of the work of the historians of the Imperial period are readily available (for example in the final chapter of Tim Duff's book *The Greek and Roman Historians* in this series) and for that reason I have chosen not to examine any of the texts just mentioned at great length. Instead, I want to focus in this chapter in particular on the interface between historical and geographical writing. Many of the texts listed above have a geographical or ethnographical dimension. That nexus of interests of course looks back at least to Herodotus' *Histories*, written in the fifth century BCE, which combines historical analysis of the Persian wars with ethnographic accounts of the various barbarian cultures of the Mediterranean world, but it seems to reach a new level of intensity in this period. For example, Appian's text, as already noted, takes a region-by-region approach. Arrian's writing on Alexander shows a particular fascination with the territories conquered by Alexander and the oddities encountered along the way; and some of his other works seem to have had a similar focus on place. For example he is said to have written a *History of Parthia*, drawing on his own experience as a general on campaign against the Parthians, and a work describing the voyage from India to the Persian city of Susa made by Alexander's friend Nearchos. We also have another surviving work entitled the *Circumnavigation of the Black Sea*, describing his travels on official business during his time as a Roman governor of Cappadocia (now central Turkey). Conversely geographical descriptions often seem unable to resist the lure of recording historical knowledge. Talking about landscape in Roman Greece often seems to involve one in exploring the rich historical associations lying behind particular places. My main focus here is on two authors in this latter category, Strabo and Pausanias. Strabo is a fairly typical example of the close engagement with the Roman present mentioned above; Pausanias is generally more interested in ignoring the Roman present, although even for him it leaves its mark. Both of those authors also, as it happens, show strong affinities with the encyclopaedic and miscellanistic techniques of composition outlined in the previous chapter: another sign of the wide spread of the knowledge-ordering obsessions of this period. Indeed some geographical writing from this period belongs more naturally in the previous chapter, in particular the work of Ptolemy, whose geographical texts are technical and heavily mathematical works less concerned with historical texture.

Strabo

First, Strabo. One of the things which is immediately striking about Strabo's work is the way in which he lays claim to a high status for his own discipline. His opening words, for example, link geography and philosophy:

> The science of geography, which I have chosen to investigate in this work, is, I think, just as much as any other discipline, a part of the business of the philosopher … Wide learning, which is the only thing which makes it possible to undertake this task, belongs only to the man who examines both human and divine affairs, understanding of which, they say, constitutes philosophy. (1.1.1)

There is perhaps a degree of ingenuity and paradox in this linking of philosophy with geography, and one might also feel that the vagueness of Strabo's claim here detracts from its plausibility, but as for Galen it is certainly not a claim made lightly. Strabo was a Stoic, and his Stoic conception of the interlinking between humankind and the universe saturates his geographical vision. In what follows he also lays claim to Homer as 'the founder of the discipline of geography' (1.1.2). This co-opting of Homer is on some level (like the link with philosophy) a conventional claim made by adherents to a number of other intellectual disciplines, with varying degrees of plausibility and ingenuity (for example we saw in Chapter 4 that Maximus of Tyre attempts in one of his orations to claim Homer as the first philosopher). But once again it is far from being an empty claim: Strabo offers several pages of thoughtful discussion on Homer as a witness to early Greek geographical knowledge. In doing so he uses Homer not so much as a source in any modern historical sense, but more as a resource, a spring-board for displaying and testing out his own geographical expertise, in much the same way as Plutarch's sympotic speakers, discussed in Chapter 5, quote from and interpret the authors of the past creatively, using them as starting-points for performing their own conversational and philosophical skills. Strabo is, in fact, not unaware of the difficulty of using Homer as a geographical source: he suggests at 8.3.23 that knowledge of the Homeric poems, and belief in their authority, is so widespread that it makes it all the more urgent to measure up his conceptions of the world against modern geographical knowledge.

However, Strabo's sense of the high status of his work may be a result not just of his awareness of the prestigious traditions of intellectual enquiry in which he is working, but also of geography's capacity to have significance for the political world of the present day. Strabo is chronologically one of the earliest of the writers studied in this book: he lived through the transition from the Roman Republic to the Principate, usually dated to 31 BCE. Most of his work was probably written up after that date. His *Geography*, too, stands halfway between the old world and the new. Books 4-17 of the work deal with the different regions of the known world in turn, moving in roughly clockwise direction around the Mediterranean, starting from Gaul and Britain and finishing in North Africa. Throughout those books we repeatedly see Strabo's interest in discussing the way in which the past marks the landscape of the present; and also his interest in looking both at the Roman present and at the pre-Roman past which lies behind it. There are hints of admiration for Roman rule. Quite often he uses the phrase 'in our time' to describe the Roman present, the period from the beginning of Roman control over the Greek east. His vision of his own work as a universal geography is closely tied to his understanding of Rome's empire as a unifying force for nearly the whole of the inhabited world. This sympathy with the Roman Empire in many ways anticipates what we see from men like Appian and Arrian and Cassius Dio. The new Augustan regime Strabo was working under exploited images of geographical dominance to glorify Roman rule over the Mediterranean world; and of course geographical knowledge was crucial in purely practical terms in allowing Rome to rule its vast empire, retaining administrative and financial control. In that sense, we might see Strabo as a pro-Augustan writer, bolstering, and in turn influenced by, Augustan ideals of Roman territorial mastery.

At the same time, however, there is also a strong sense in Strabo's work of independence from Roman ways of seeing the world, and a dependence on pre-Roman ways of understanding geography. For example, it is clear – not least from the prefatory claims I have mentioned above – that he is working primarily within a Greek frame, taking part in an enterprise which dates back long before the first contacts between Greece and Rome. That Hellenic framework is made obvious in his long (and largely critical) discussion of the great Hellenistic geographer Eratosthenes, which occupies much of the first two of the text's seventeen books. Moreover, when he states, early on in the work, that 'the empire of the Romans and of the Parthians has contributed quite a lot to this kind of practical knowledge for the geographers of today, just as the expedition of Alexander, as Eratosthenes points out, made an enormous contribution to the geographers of the past' (1.2.1), he is both acknowledging the importance of Roman rule as a vehicle for expansion of our understanding of the world and also taking a slightly stand-offish position in relation to it. In other words, he shows an awareness of the fact that Rome's dominance is only one element in the much broader and longer story of developing human understanding of geographical space (although see also 11.6.4 for Strabo's doubts about the accuracy of accounts of Alexander's expedition, by comparison with more recent Roman and Parthian information).

Pausanias and the Greek past

For Pausanias, writing roughly a century and a half later in the mid second century CE, the sense of a virtual world of history and myth lying behind the surface of the present-day Greek landscape is even more conspicuous. Strabo never comes close to matching the depth of Pausanias' obsession with local history and local landscape. In the past Pausanias' work has sometimes been categorised as a travel guide, but in reality it is very much more than that: it is a work which, like so many of the other texts from this period examined in earlier chapters, offers us a fantasy of access to the past. Pausanias holds out the promise of seeing beyond the traces of the past we encounter in the present day, providing us with a glimpse of the vast network of interlinking stories which make up the Greek historical heritage. In line with that objective, his work is focused exclusively on the oldest part of the Greek-speaking world, that is the Greek mainland, despite the fact that he came from Asia Minor himself. Mainland Greece may have been economically weak by comparison with the thriving cities of Asia Minor, but it still occupied a key imaginative space within the collective Greek (and Roman) psyche as a place connected with the former glory of the Greek world.

Take, for example, the very opening section of the work as it survives, describing the sights which greet a visitor on arrival in the territory of Attica:

On the Greek mainland, facing the islands of the Cyclades and the Aegean sea, Cape Sounion juts out from the land of Attica. If you sail around the cape you come to a harbour and a temple to Athene of Sounion on the point of the cape. If you sail on you come to Laurion, where once the Athenians had silver mines, and a deserted island, not big, called the Island of Patroklos; for Patroklos built a fortification on it, and a palisade. He was admiral of the Egyptian triremes sent by Ptolemy, son of Ptolemy, son of Lagos to help the Athenians, when Antigonos the son of Demetrios was ravaging the land, having invaded with an army, and at the same time was blockading them with a fleet from the sea. Piraeus was a district from early times, but it was not a harbour before the time when Themistokles was *archon* in Athens. Instead their port was Phaleron, for this is the place where the sea is least far away from the city, and it is from here that they say Mnestheus set sail to Troy with the ships, and before that Theseus set off to pay Minos the penalty for the death of Androgeos.

This is a curiously abrupt opening: none of Strabo's self-justifying prefatory rhetoric here. Some scholars think that Pausanias' preface is missing from the text, but this opening is in many ways appropriate to everything which follows. Pausanias confronts us in these opening lines with the specifics of a particular local landscape: that is the enduring fascination of his work. And although he does generalise once about the idea that his work aims to encompass 'all Greek things' (*panta ta hellenika*) (1.26.4), a phrase which on one reading seems to point towards an ambition to encompass the whole of the Greek cultural heritage, it is striking that Pausanias achieves that aim only through attention to detail, rarely stepping back from his on-the-ground focus.

In the passage quoted we see a typical example of the way in which each of the places Pausanias visits carries traces of the historical and mythical past, for those who know how to look. In this case there is an impression, as we read, of moving further and further back into the distant past: we hear first of the conflicts of the Hellenistic world, in this case the capture of Athens by the Macedonian king Antigonos in the mid-third century BCE. From there we move back to the classical world of the early fifth century, and to the contribution of Themistokles, who was instrumental in turning Athens into a great naval power (and in the development of the Piraeus as a harbour, as Pausanias makes clear), and was one of the architects of the Athenian victory over Persia, which was so often viewed in later centuries as one of the founding moments of Greek greatness. And then from there we delve ever deeper into the world of myth – of Theseus and the Trojan wars. There is no clear-cut distinction between history and myth in Pausanias' conception. All of these different periods of history crowd together, clamouring for attention as Pausanias views the sites with which they are linked.

Typical also in this passage is the way in which he tends to start on the edge of each of the territories of Greece he examines, moving gradually to the centre: as Book 1 proceeds we move closer and closer to the centre of the city of Athens. That movement is echoed in the structure of his work as a whole, which focuses in Books 5 and 6 on the territory of Olympia, home to the oldest of the Greek festivals (the Olympics were said to have been founded in 776 BCE), and a place filled with reminders of the past through the vast number of commemorative statues which were dotted around the sanctuary. 'There are', he tells us 'many other things one can see or hear about among the Greeks which are worthy of amazement. But the things done in Eleusis [i.e. the home of the Eleusinian mystery cult near Athens] and the contest in Olympia, these have the greatest share of divine attention' (5.10.1).

Pausanias and the Roman present

One of Pausanias' attractions, for many modern readers, has been the promise of an eye-witness account of Greece in the Roman period. Others have been keen to measure up his account against the sites of ancient Greece as they stand today, and if you travel to these sites you may still see an occasional tourist reading eagerly from Pausanias. We need to be careful, however, about assuming that Pausanias is offering us a complete picture. For one thing, if we assume that Pausanias' main aim is the writing of accurate site reports or tourist guides we rather miss the point: he is interested above all in the stories which the landscape gives him access to, and with that in mind it would hardly be surprising to see him being selective and even at times vague about detail. To be more specific, one of the immediately striking things about his account is the fact that it is mainly concerned with ancient monuments; more recent buildings and statues, from the Roman period, are less often mentioned. We know, for example, that the site at Olympia had a number of very conspicuous recent monuments – for example the Nymphaion (a monumental fountain) built by Herodes Atticus – at the time when Pausanias visited (probably the 160s or 170s). Pausanias passes over them in silence, as if the presence of the more distant past is so powerful in this place that it drowns out more recent buildings. We also find a number of barbed comments about Roman intervention in Greece, and about a number of individual Roman emperors. In that sense he adopts a very different approach from Strabo, whose acknowledgement and even at times approval of the Roman Empire in some ways has more in common with Hellenistic predecessors like Polybius than with the more aggressively and exclusively Hellenic authors of the second century.

That is not to say, however, that Pausanias is uninterested in Rome and entirely unwilling to praise what it has brought. Where a Roman-period monument is great enough to be worthy of mention it gets full attention. In his account of Athens, for example, we read descriptions of the temple of Olympian Zeus, completed by the emperor Hadrian not many decades before Pausanias' visit, and of the marble athletic stadium built even more recently by Herodes Atticus (already mentioned in Chapter 3). Both of those sites stand close to each other in to the south-east of the historic centre of Athens. Of the former, he speaks as follows:

> Hadrian the Roman emperor dedicated both the temple and the statue, which is worth seeing: all other statues alike, apart from the colossi at Rhodes and at Rome, fall short of it in size; it is made from ivory and gold, and it shows considerable skill, if you think of the size of it. (1.18.6)

Hadrian seems to come in for special praise from Pausanias both here and elsewhere, thanks no doubt to his sponsorship of Greek culture. That apparently innocuous phrase 'worth noticing' is one other key to Pausanias' principles of selection: elsewhere in the work he several times echoes Herodotus' claim, in the preface of Book 1 of his *Histories*, that he is interested in recording 'great and amazing deeds'. And Pausanias seems quite willing to include very special Roman-period monuments in this category, as if to demonstrate the way in which the building projects of the post-classical world he inhabits can sometimes match, simply by their size, if not by any claim to historical significance, the ruins and survivals of pre-Roman culture.

There is a similar effect in his very brief mention of Herodes Atticus' stadium:

> A thing which is not so attractive to hear about but wonderful to look at, is the stadium of white marble. The best way of bearing witness to the size of it is to describe how the hill, starting from a crescent shape high above the Ilissos, stretches down in straight double lines to the bank of the river. This stadium was built by the Athenian man Herodes, and most of the Pentelic quarry was used up by him in the construction. (1.19.6)

Here, in contrast with the Nymphaion at Olympia, the stadium is visually breathtaking enough to force its way into Pausanias' list of marvels despite his disapproval of Herodes Atticus. The negative comment here is hard to decipher precisely, but the final detail about the consumption of the Pentelic quarry suggests that one of Pausanias' worries is the way in which Herodes' modern building works have the potential to do violence to the landscape of Greece (Herodes was also renowned for having wished, like the emperor Nero, to cut a canal through the Isthmus of Corinth, an act which is sometimes represented as a sign of superhuman arrogance). Interestingly, however, there are signs elsewhere that Pausanias is confident in the capacity of the Greek landscape to survive whatever the Roman world can throw at it. Immediately after his account of Hadrian's temple of Olympian Zeus, for example, he tell us that

> these are the antiquities in the temple precinct: a bronze statue of Zeus and a temple of Kronos and Rhea and an area of land sacred to Olympian Earth. Here the ground has split apart to the width of about two feet, and they say that after the deluge in the time of Deukalion, the water ran away here underground. (1.18.7)

The Greek mythical story of the survival of Deukalion after a great flood roughly parallels the Old Testament story of Noah. Here too the land is split or damaged, but in this case Pausanias seems to hint at a more positive interpretation: the landscape still carries the marks of ancient myth and history whatever is built on top of it, still has its own independent identity regardless of later interference.

It is important to stress, in summary, that Pausanias is not straightforwardly hostile to and/or neglectful of Rome and of the modern world. One might even argue that Roman rule is the very thing which makes his vision of Greece possible, allowing him to look back to the past from the unifying perspective of the Roman present, after the end of independent Greek history, tracing the signs of the past in the ruins it has left behind for the present day. In that sense he is closer to Strabo than he initially seems. His primary interest is undeniably in the pre-Roman Greek world. Nevertheless his work is a good example of the way in which the literature of this period, and historical writing in particular, for all its obsession with the past, sometimes turns out to be more closely engaged with the Roman present than initially appears to be the case.

Chapter 7

Biography

Biography and emperors

We have seen that one of the recurring characteristics of the literature of the Roman Empire (in Greek and indeed in Latin) is an interest in accumulation of knowledge. One might similarly make a case for biography as a distinctive preoccupation of the Imperial period. Biography seems to have emerged from the habits of praising individuals for their life and achievements through the conventions of epideictic oratory – and those habits of praise were of course embedded in Greek and Roman political life well before the Roman period. There are examples of biographical writing dating back at least as far as Xenophon's *Cyropaedia*, his early fourth-century BCE description of the life and education of the Persian king Cyrus. Nevertheless, there is a marked increase in charting great lives in the first century CE and after. In some cases that biographical enterprise itself takes on a compilatory framework, for example in Diogenes Laertius' *Lives of the Philosophers* or in Philostratus' *Lives of the Sophists*, both of which we will turn to later, and both of which cover in turn many different exponents of their respective fields. That kind of encyclopaedic or miscellanistic approach to biography, accumulating different biographical subjects, and heaping together anecdotes to illustrate each individual's character and achievements, makes these biographical writings very much of their time (although an interest in collecting brief anecdotes to illustrate virtue or vice dates right back to Aristotle and his contemporaries in the fourth century).

One driving force for this biographical turn may be the politics of Rome. The Roman Republic had increasingly seen vast concentrations of power in the hands of a few individuals; and from the reign of Augustus onwards a monopoly of power and prestige by individual emperors. Some biographical texts deal with the emperors directly: for example, Suetonius' *Lives of the Caesars* in Latin (written in the early second century), and the more sensationalistic and unreliable Latin biographies of the *Historia Augusta*, probably by various authors, which carry on the story from the life of Hadrian, where Suetonius left off (some or all of the texts of the *Historia Augusta* may have been composed in the fourth century or after). We also have evidence for imperial autobiography. Augustus is said to have written memoirs; and his lengthy account of his own achievements, the *Res Gestae*, which was inscribed as a public monument in many sites across the empire, also has a strongly autobiographical character. One might even view Julius Caesar's *Gallic War*, his account of his campaigns in Gaul, as an enterprise of autobiographical self-justification, despite its dispassionate, military-historical character (he refers to himself throughout in the third person). In other cases the importance of the emperors makes its mark on biographical writing more obliquely: as we shall see from the examples discussed below, great men are often described in terms which imply that their influence imitates or even rivals that of the emperor.

Plutarch

My first example, Plutarch, is probably the most famous and most read of all the Imperial-period biographers. In some respects he is typical of these trends. His vast project of biographical writing included lives of the emperors, although only two of those – *Galba* and *Otho* – survive. Most of his surviving biographical writing, however, takes a more oblique approach to the Principate. He tends to avoid explicit reference to the emperors. His pairing of Greek and Roman subjects does indeed imply questions with urgent contemporary relevance about the capacity of Greek education to civilise and guide Roman power, but he addresses that question by dealing with figures from Republican Rome and Hellenistic Greece and before.

One of the other things that makes his work stand out is the fact that he has an unusually intense interest in the biographical representation of virtue. It is clear for Suetonius and others that moral judgement does matter in assessing an emperor's worth. That is implied by Suetonius' fascination with the private lives of his subjects. Even more so than for our own tabloid-driven media, ancient biography is obsessed with the idea that private morality gives a window on to a politician's fitness to rule. Plutarch, however, takes this assumption to a much further extreme. For him, biography is essentially a philosophical, moralising enterprise, one half of the lifelong philosophical project to which his other works, grouped together as the *Moralia*, also contribute. He takes a Platonic view of the human soul, which assumes a split between two elements – the passionate and the rational – and stresses the importance of bringing the former under the control of the latter (as Tim Duff has shown – see Further reading). For Plutarch, Greek education is the most powerful means of achieving that end. The degree to which each of his subjects has succeeded in that kind of spiritual balance is his key interest – even more important ultimately than any judgement about political or military success. That question underlies all of his painstaking historical research and vivid story-telling which have made these works so important for modern understanding of major historical figures from Greek and Roman history.

There is space here for just one example from that vast corpus, from the *Life of Antony*. Antony, the opponent of Octavian (later the emperor Augustus) in the Roman civil wars of the 30s BCE, defeated at the battle of Actium along with his lover the Egyptian queen Cleopatra, was painted by his enemies as a man of monstrous passions. Cicero in the 40s BCE had denounced him in these terms; Octavian's victory over him was helped by his ability to paint Antony as a figure whose passion for a foreign queen would overturn the order of the Roman state. Given that reputation it is not difficult to see his attractions as a biographical subject for Plutarch. What Plutarch does is to offer us an anatomy of his passions, showing us how Antony at times succeeds in overcoming the natural passion of his soul, and then how it finally destroys him. Take, for example, the following passage, describing Antony's first approaches to Cleopatra:

> Being of such a kind in his nature, the love for Cleopatra came upon Antony as a final evil, and awakening many of the passions which were hidden and as yet undisturbed inside him, and whipping them into a frenzy (*anabakcheusas*), managed to annihilate and destroy whatever good and saving traits were still resisting. This is how he was captured (*halisketai*): … (*Antony* 25.1)

We hear in what follows that he sends an envoy to Cleopatra to complain about her support for Antony's enemy Cassius. The envoy, Dellius, impressed by Cleopatra, does his best to flatter her, and to praise Antony to her as 'the most pleasant of leaders and the most humane (*philanthrôpotaton*)' (25.3). And from there Antony's passions take control of him, and his doom advances by faster and faster steps. It is often stated that ancient writers tend to work with a conception of underlying character as something unchanging, and certainly this passage seems to support that view: Antony's destructively passionate ambition is something which always lies within him, and only needs a particular combination of circumstances to bring it into view (presumably a different path of events might have made it easier for it to stay submerged beneath the surface). Immediately clear here is the image of the soul as an almost physical, compartmentalised entity, with constant warring between its different parts. The language of excess and frenzy is prominent: the word *anabakcheusas* equates the raging of his passions with the ritual frenzy of worshippers of the god Dionysus. The word *halisketai* equates Antony's falling in love with military defeat and capture – pointedly so, given that the sentence following refers to Antony's strategic planning for the wars he is fighting ('as he was getting ready for the Parthian war'). Finally the terms of Dellius' praise of Antony are highly ironic given the unflattering anatomy of his soul which immediately precedes them: in Plutarch the adjective *philanthrôpos* (here in the superlative – *philanthrôpotaton* ('most humane')) is repeatedly used for precisely the kind of spiritual balance which Antony has just been shown to fall short of.

Diogenes Laertius

We see philosophical biography of a different kind in Diogenes Laertius' *Lives and Opinions of Eminent Philosophers*, which charts the lives of important figures in the development of philosophy over its many centuries of history, drawing heavily on Hellenistic sources. For him, too, anecdotes and peculiar stories are important: many of his subjects are eccentric figures, and made all the more memorable for that, for example in the many cases where philosophers are characterised by the peculiar manner of their deaths. Pythagoras, for example, is said on one account to have been killed by pursuers, who caught up with him when he refused to run away across a field of beans (8.39), which Pythagorean doctrine viewed as sacred, and which Pythagoras himself never ate, as the author has earlier explained (8.19). Heraclitus, in a story which reminds us of his misanthropy if not any particular feature of his philosophy, retreats to the mountains out of a hatred of humanity and lives off a diet of grass and herbs, which causes him to die from dropsy, despite his attempts to save himself by burying himself in manure in order to draw off moisture from his body (9.3). Diogenes Laertius also, however, takes quite a systematic approach to recording the philosophical principles of each of his philosophers, with Epicurus addressed last and at particular length, in the whole of Book 10, in line with Diogenes' own Epicurean allegiances. He also takes a close interest in intellectual genealogy, recording for many of these figures the teachers they have learned from, supplementing conventional biographical interest in family origins with attention to intellectual paternity.

Philostratus

In that sense Diogenes is an important representative of another major strand in Imperial-period biography, that is the urge to examine the lives of prominent figures within a particular intellectual field. Here I want to illustrate that interest by turning again to Philostratus' *Lives of the Sophists*, a text whose thematic complexity and artfulness has not always been recognised in its own right, so heavily has it been plundered as a source for information about sophistic activity in the second and third centuries.

One of the immediately striking things about Philostratus' sophists, as we have already seen in Chapter 3, is their larger-than-life character, and that goes especially for the two dominant figures of the work, whose lives are addressed at far greater length than any of the others, Polemo and Herodes Atticus. Here the texts already discussed in this chapter are useful points of comparison, and give some idea of the way in which Philostratus takes on conventional biographical motifs and twists them to innovative effect. For one thing, it is clear that both Polemo and Herodes are often being described almost in emperor-like terms, as figures whose wealth and power are so vast that they can be conceptualised only through a comparison with the emperors themselves, and which sometimes come even to rival them (although at other times it is made clear that the emperors stand far above even these most revered of intellectual figures). We hear, for example, that Polemo was renowned for having ejected from his house Antoninus the son of the emperor Marcus Aurelius, on returning from a trip to find that Antoninus had decided to invite himself to lodge there (*Lives of the Sophists* 1.25 (533-4)). Both Polemo and Herodes are also in some ways heroic, almost Homeric figures, whose extraordinary skill gives them an almost superhuman aura. For example in 1.25 (558) Philostratus tells us how Herodes threw himself to the ground through grief on the hearing of the death of his daughter, in ways which clearly recall Achilles' reaction to the death of Patroclus in the *Iliad*. The sophists' passionate, heroic natures are also clear in their rivalries with each other: at one point (1.8 (490-91)), in recounting the bitter quarrel between Polemo and Favorinus, Philostratus suggests that 'they should be forgiven for their rivalry, since human nature believes that love of glory never grows old' (although he also goes on to criticise them for some of the more personal insults against one another). The contrast with Plutarch is fascinating. Philostratus, like Plutarch, is fascinated by passion, and by the image of emotions of anger and lust for glory running out of control. But unlike Plutarch he declines, except in exceptional cases, to pass judgement on those things, and we are sometimes left with the impression that the sophists' excess is precisely the thing which makes them great, by raising them above the normal human level, and making them hard to fit into the normal workings of human society.

Some of this is typical of other biographies of intellectual and indeed religious figures in the Roman world, as we shall see further in a moment, but it is important to stress that Philostratus' approach to biography is very unusual, and determined in part by his own sophistic perspective: he was himself a sophist, and we get occasional glimpses of his own friendships and professional relationships and rivalries with those he describes. I focus here on just one example of his curiously sophistic take on bio-graphical conventions, that is his fascination with the speaking voices of his subjects, another feature we have already glimpsed in Chapter 3. It is not unusual in ancient biography to find passages of physical description, drawing on the language of physiognomy. Philostratus follows that trend, but in addition he gives intricate accounts of the speaking voice and performance style of each of his subjects. He tells us, for example, of Favorinus, that 'his voice sounded shrill, weak, and strained, the kind of voice that nature gives to eunuchs' (*Lives of the Sophists* 1.8 (489)); that 'his style of speech was careless, but also learned and pleasant; he was said to improvise with fluency' (491); and that 'when he spoke in Rome, there was universal interest, to the extent that even those who did not understand the Greek language took pleasure from listening, for he beguiled them with the sound of his voice and the expressiveness of his glance and the rhythm of his speech' (491). Polemo's eloquence was 'passionate and combative and clear in sound, like the Olympic trumpet, and the Demosthenic character of his opinions gives it special distinction, and the impressiveness of his delivery is not tedious, but bright and inspired, as if delivered by an oracle' (1.25 (542)). Favorinus and Polemo are exceptional cases, but there are similar passages of description for most of Philostratus' sophists. The implication seems to be that every individual voice is different, and that each is intricately linked with the broader character of its speaker, just as (on the account of ancient physiognomists like Polemo himself) an individual's physical appearance offers a window on to his or her vices and virtues.

In Polemo's case Philostratus' focus on sophistic voice reaches per-haps its most extraordinary peak, with the description of his death. Philostratus recounts a number of different variant versions of Polemo's burial place, in the process painting Polemo once again as a heroic figure – the burial place of a hero in ancient hero cult had particular significance – and then gives his own preferred version:

But this version is closer to the truth, that he is buried in Laodikeia near to the Syrian gate, where the tombs of his ancestors also stand, and that he was buried while still alive, for he had given this instruction to those closest to him, and that as he lay in the grave he urged on those who were shutting it up, saying, 'Hurry, hurry, may the sun not see me reduced to silence'. And to his lamenting relatives, he shouted out, 'Give me a body, and I will declaim.' (1.25 (543-4))

This is a particularly startling version of the biographical convention mentioned above for Diogenes Laertius that the manner of a person's death often gives us one of the most powerful ways of understanding his life. It is typical, too, of Philostratus' interest in monumentalisation. Many of the sophists themselves received honorary statues and inscriptions in the cites of the east of the empire. Polemo, in this case, is such a prodigious figure that he becomes a part of his own monument even during the final moment of his own life. In addition, however, it gives us a remarkable image of the centrality of the voice for a sophist's fame and indeed his very being. Polemo's voice is ensured immortality here: even as it is muffled by the spadefuls of earth it ensures its own capacity to reverberate through future ages thanks to Philostratus' own work, which is itself a monument to sophistic glory. The voice of the sophist, unlike the achievements of other literary artists, disappears even as it is spoken. Philostratus responds to his own anxiety about that evanescence by attempting to set their voices in stone, and to preserve them for future ages.

Christian biography

Philostratus' interest in portraying the sophists as charismatic, at times almost superhuman figures makes his biography very much of its time. Increasingly through the Roman period there is a tendency to celebrate the lives and powers of philosophers and holy men as figures who have a special access to the divine world. Philostratus' other great biographical work, his *Life of Apollonius of Tyana*, is a good example, portraying the famous Pythagorean philosopher as a vehicle for divine wisdom, with powers of miracle working. Christian biographical writing plays an important role in that trend, both influencing and influenced by its Greco-Roman equivalents. The gospels are themselves close in some ways to Greco-Roman biographical conventions. And the development is greatly intensified in the genre of hagiography or saints lives, which first comes into being in the mid-third century. Ascetic saints – devoted to fasting and self-denial – became increasingly familiar figures in the landscape of the Christian empire from the fourth century onwards. Their influence and fame came in part from the extraordinary stories of inhuman endurance and miracle-working associated with them, but also, connected with that, from widespread assumptions about their capacity to bridge the gap between human and divine. Full discussion of the Christian literature of the fourth century and after is beyond the scope of this book. Moreover, it is important to stress that not all Christian biography centres around these kinds of charismatic holy figures: Eusebius' *Life of Constantine* which charted (among other things) the accession of Constantine to the throne, his conversion to Christianity, and his later religious policy, is a case in point. My point for now is simply that Philostratus' biographies of the sophists are distant and early ancestors of the prodigious and often controversial figures who fill the pages of early Christian hagiography. One might even see the differences between Plutarch's moralising and Philostratus' heroising as symptomatic of those shifting cultural currents, given that Philostratus was writing more than a century later – although it is important not to oversimplify in making that claim, since the idea of the philosopher as holy man dates back many centuries, even if it gains a new intensity in the period we are looking at here.

Lucian

Even half a century before Philostratus, Lucian offers two brilliant parodies of precisely these traditions of divinely inspired holy men and philosophers, in his *Alexander* and *Peregrinus*, which form the final focus for this chapter. Both Alexander and Peregrinus were real people, contemporaries of Lucian who attracted a wide following, and who claimed special abilities to communicate with the gods. Alexander set up a cult in honour of the god Asklepios, worshipped in the form of a snake named Glykon, and gave out oracles on the god's behalf. Peregrinus burned himself to death at the Olympic games, ostensibly (as far as we can tell) as a gesture of his own philosophical indifference to bodily suffering. Lucian exposes both of them as frauds. These two anti-biographies are counter-balanced by another positive biographical work, the *Demonax*, which characterises the philosopher Demonax as a figure who stands out against all sophistic flashiness and quasi-magical self-presentation. Demonax specialises in brief, witty putdowns designed to puncture pretension, and is described being very rude to both Peregrinus and Herodes Atticus (who were themselves bitter enemies, partly perhaps because they were fighting for some of the same space as charismatic intellectuals).

Demonax offers us a mirror image of Alexander and Peregrinus, making their deceptiveness and ambition seem all the more horrifying and absurd by comparison.

Lucian's debunking of these two figures works in part by subverting the usual structures and motifs of biographical writing. That is a surprisingly unusual move: the origins of biographical writing in encomiastic (i.e. praise) oration still had great influence, and it is difficult to find parallels in ancient literature for this kind of anti-biography. There is one complicating factor, however, in viewing these works as straightforward attempts at denunciation and that is the way in which Lucian subtly associates himself with both of these figures even as he denounces them, advertising his own skills of deceptive self-dramatisation, and his own ability to beat them at their own game. In that sense the writing of biography, for Lucian, as for Philostratus (who draws attention several times to his own involvement in professional sophistic rivalries), is always also autobiography.

First, the *Peregrinus* – or to give it its full title, *On the Death of Peregrinus*. That title immediately signals the work's undermining of traditional biography, replacing the usual titular word 'Life' with 'Death'. It also signals that Peregrinus is a supreme example of the pattern already discussed whereby death becomes a defining moment of life in biographical writing. Suicide seems to have been an acceptable manner of death within many different philosophical systems in the ancient world, and many famous philosophers are praised in Diogenes Laertius and elsewhere for the way in which their suicides demonstrate their philosophical equanimity and their lack of attachment to the things of the world. Lucian's strategy is to stamp out any sympathy for Peregrinus' attempt to categorise himself in similar terms: Peregrinus, he stresses over and over again, is driven above all by the desire for glory, which makes him about as far removed from the famous philosophical suicides of the past as one could imagine. On Lucian's account, at least, Peregrinus seems to have made a very concerted attempt to associate himself with a set of great figures from myth and from the philosophical past, but he goes through so many different models that he ends up not doing justice to any of them, in fact he ends up perverting and debasing all of the precedents he lays his hands on. His primary identification is as a Cynic philosopher, and in line with that he portrays himself as a Herakles figure – the hero Herakles, who was burned to death as a release from poisoning, and whose soul was translated to Olympus, was often taken as an icon of self-control and philosophical virtue. But he also associates himself at various times with Socrates, with Christianity – Lucian describes how he joins a set of gullible Christians at one point in his life (*Peregrinus* 11-16) – and with the eastern wisdom of the Indian wise men, the Brahmans, who were said to burn themselves to death as a sign of their detachment from the things of the body (indeed one Brahman sage is said to have done precisely that in Rome during the reign of Augustus).

The final moment of burning, held some time after the Olympic festival, and well outside the main Olympic site, is comically anti-climactic. Peregrinus puts it off for so long, out of fear, that many of the spectators turn out to have gone home. The moment of suicide is described in insultingly matter-of-fact terms, which themselves subvert Peregrinus' bid for glory. Lucian's response is to laugh: the language of laughter saturates this text, an appropriate reaction, one might think, to the images of theatricality which are applied repeatedly to Peregrinus' planning. Peregrinus wants his life to have the dignity of tragedy; Lucian sees only what is comic.

This opposition between Lucian and Peregrinus is slyly undermined, however, in the closing section of the work. Many people, Lucian tells us, got the time of the self-immolation wrong, and came too late. As Lucian returns to the sanctuary of Olympia he meets some of these people and gives them an account of what has happened:

> If I saw someone who looked serious, I would tell him the whole story without adornment just as I am doing to you, but to the fools who were desperate to hear, I dramatised (*etragôdoun*) things a little on my own account ... (39)

claiming, for example, that the moment of Peregrinus' death was accompanied by an earthquake, and that a vulture flew up out of the middle of the pyre going up to heaven. Later he meets another, respectable looking man who repeats back to him the detail of the vulture, swearing that he saw it with his own eyes. Lucian is here flaunting his own command of theatrical trickery, with the implication that it is vastly superior to Peregrinus' absurd and incompetent version: the word *etragôdoun* ('dramatised') is a verb used several times for Peregrinus himself earlier in the work.

In Alexander of Abonuteichos Lucian finds an altogether more formidable opponent. As for Peregrinus, we know that Alexander was a real person: in fact he seems to have been very much more successful than Peregrinus in his attempts to set himself up as a powerful and influential religious figure. For example, a number of coins and statues have been found in different parts of Asia Minor depicting the snake-god Glykon already mentioned (an image of Glykon on a coin is depicted on the front cover of this book). There are times, in fact, when Lucian comes close to expressing admiration for Alexander via conventional language of bio-graphical praise. For example he seems to have some of the same physical presence and quasi-divine beauty as Philostratus' sophists: 'His eyes', we hear, 'shone with great vehemence, as if divinely inspired; his voice was at the same time very sweet and very clear' (*Alexander* 3). His intellectual virtues are similarly outstanding: 'in intelligence and shrewdness and sharpness he stood far above everyone else; and in his curiosity of mind and his quickness at learning and his memory and his natural readiness to study – he had all these things in every case to excess. But he used them in the worst possible way …' (4). That awareness of Alexander's gifts runs right through everything which follows. Even when Lucian himself joins the story, publicly biting the prophet's hand instead of shaking it, as a gesture of contempt when he is granted an audience (55), it is hard to avoid the impression that they may be on some level kindred spirits. Immediately after this incident Lucian even accepts Alexander's offer of friendship, although he claims later that this is simply out of self-defence, to protect himself from the fury of Alexander's followers.

At times it even seems that the problem lies just as much with the gullibility of his audience as with Alexander himself. Take, for example, the following passage, from the moment where Alexander begins to fake the discovery of the god Asklepios:

> In the morning, he went out naked into the *agora* (i.e. the central public space of the city) having just a golden loincloth covering his genitals, and carrying his sickle and shaking his hair, like those devotees of the mother goddess who collect money and go about in a state of inspiration, and leaping up on top of an altar he began ranting and pronounced the city blessed because it was about to receive the god in person. Those who were present – for almost the whole city had flocked there, including women and old men and children – were astonished and they praised and bowed down. And he, speaking in unclear words, the kind which might have been Hebrew or Phoenician, amazed these people even though he did not know what he was saying, except that he mixed in the names Apollo and Asklepios into everything he said. (13)

Here Alexander is taking advantage of the chance to claim direct access to the divine sphere: his imitation of the trance state of eastern cult is one first sign for his onlookers of what to expect; and their expectations of a window opening up between the human and divine are richly rewarded in what follows. Alexander finds an egg in the foundations of a temple under construction, and inside it a tiny baby snake, which grows in just a few days (so he pretends) to adult size, and which he claims is the god descended to earth to bring blessings to the city.

The whole thing, of course is faked: Alexander has planted the egg the day before, having carefully put the baby snake inside and glued it back together again. He then substitutes it for an adult snake during the days which follow. When the people come to see the god he keeps the real snake's head tucked under his arm, and displays instead a fake snake's head made of cloth, with a puppet mouth, in order to trick people into thinking it is real (15). The gullibility of the people who fail to spot that trick is prefigured in the passage just quoted. Lucian stresses their amazement in terms which give an impression of unanimity: the whole city thinks as one, as if incapable of individual reflection. The final details in this passage about Alexander's capacity to beguile the audience despite their lack of understanding is another sign of Lucian's play with the motifs which are common in biographies of charismatic intellectual and religious figures: both Favorinus (in the passage quoted above) and Dio of Prusa (*Lives of the Sophists* 1.7 (488)) are said by Philostratus to have been able to beguile even those who did not understand their Greek, or (in the case of Dio) those who did not have a full grounding in Greek culture; and we might even think of the Acts of the Apostles as a parallel here, where the apostles are granted the gift of speaking in tongues and so communicating with all nations (Acts 2.1-13). Alexander's self-dramatisation is a debased and fake version of those motifs.

Moreover, as for other charismatic figures his powers of communication and inspiration work not just in person, but also come to have almost a global reach: the vast network of informers and envoys and messengers Alexander develops are portrayed in quasi-imperial terms:

> everywhere in the Roman empire he sent soothsayers, warning the cities to be on their guard against famine and fires and earthquakes; and he himself promised to them that he would give them infallible aid, to prevent any of these things from happening ... In Rome itself he posted a great many of his fellow-conspirator as spies, who reported everyone's opinions to him and gave advance information about the questions they would put to Alexander, and about what they most desired, so that he would be ready with his answers even before the messengers arrived. (36-7)

Once again, as for Philostratus' sophists, and even for Plutarch, with his interest in the civilising effect of Greek culture on Roman military and political leaders, the figure of the emperor becomes a crucial reference-point for the Roman Empire's fascination with biography.

Chapter 8

Conclusion: Poetry and Prose

The most conspicuous gap in this book so far, especially for anyone used to pre-Roman Greek literature, or indeed to Latin literature, is poetry. The Imperial period was an age of prose. To some extent the dominance of prose is due to the taste of later ages, who for whatever reason chose not to preserve the period's poetic productions or to view them as influential. But it is undeniable that even at the time, for the readers of the first to third centuries, prose writing had a much more exclusive monopoly on literary prestige than ever before. The writers we have looked at so far were famous in their lifetimes because of their prose creations.

That said, there is a danger of underestimating the degree to which poetry continued to hold an integral role in the elite culture of the period. Even if verse was rarely viewed as a vehicle for great literary ambitions, it is clear that not only a knowledge of earlier poetry but also a facility with poetic composition was viewed as a standard accomplishment for any educated person. For example, many sophists are known to have composed poetry: most notably, we have a number of surviving epigrams by Herodes Atticus. The cultural prominence of poetry becomes all the more clear when we look at the epigraphic record, which gives details for musical and poetic contests, including contests involving performance of original poetic compositions, held in religious festivals – often alongside athletic competition – throughout the Greek world.

The genre of epigram was particularly popular – and particularly suitable to amateur dabbling as well as professional composition. Epigrams are small poems, sometimes composed to be engraved on statue bases or gravestones, but also, and increasingly so from the Hellenistic period onwards, intended to be free-standing examples of literary ingenuity. Often we find a twist in the final line, or else an interest in compressed or paradoxical expression. The epigram seems to have been particularly associated with the context of the symposium, with its tradition of ingenious speech, and some accordingly focus on highly traditional sympotic subject matter like love and drinking. There is also, however, an increasingly prominent fashion in the Imperial period for satirical epigram. In particular the first-century Greek poet Lucillius, who was imitated by the

Latin satirical epigrammatist Martial, devotes many verses to satire of contemporary life. Some, for example, deal with the contemporary craze for athletics. In the two epigrams following, for example, he mocks boxers who have been scarred almost beyond recognition by their fighting (the Greeks fought with hardened leather strips wound round their fists instead of boxing gloves):

> When Odysseus returned safely to his homeland after twenty years Argos the dog recognised his appearance as soon as he saw him. But you, Stratophon, after boxing for four hours, have become unrecognisable not just to dogs, but to the city. If you wish to look at your own face in a mirror, you will yourself say on oath, 'I am not Stratophon'. (*Greek Anthology* 11.77)

> Your head, Apollophanes, has become a sieve, like the lower edges of moth-eaten booklets, exactly like ant-holes, both slanting and straight, like musical notes, Lydian and Phrygian. But you might as well carry on boxing without fear; for even if you get hit on the head, you will still look the same, keeping the the scars you already have; for it would be impossible to have any more. (*Greek Anthology* 11.78)

Many epigrams show particular fascination with small-scale objects – mice and mosquitoes, to name just two traditional examples. These small objects often seem to stand for the smallness of the genre itself, allowing the epigrammatist to comment self-reflexively on the literary act in which he is engaged. In Lucillius' case, by contrast, the joke lies partly in the monstrously oversized and inelegant character of the overmuscled and ugly athletes he lampoons, who are humorously inappropriate to the elegant smallness of the epigram form.

Many of the epigrams which survive, including most of those carved on stone, are anonymous. Anonymity may be part of the attraction in some cases, implying as it does the ephemeral character of the text: they offer us the tantalising pleasure of listening to snatches of conversation and to voices which cannot be fully identified or contextualised. But that anonymous character also contributes to the unlikelihood of epigram being viewed as a vehicle for serious literary fame. Nevertheless many of the authors are named, and we can in some cases build up a sense of a single epigrammatist with distinctive preoccupations and themes running through a single body of work. The most important source of named epigrams (although it also itself contains many anonymous texts) is the *Palatine Anthology*, a vast collection assembled in the tenth century, but drawing on earlier collections put together in the Imperial period. The fact that one of the named authors of the *Anthology* is Lucian is significant, another reminder that we should not see a clear split between poetry and prose. Many of the great literary and sophistic figures of the period clearly had the ability not only to quote from earlier poetry, but also to throw together their own verses in the appropriate situation.

Melic (lyric) poetry – that is poetry written for (or as if for) musical performance, either by individuals or by choirs (especially in hymns to the gods) – was also an important feature of the poetic landscape of the period, although relatively little survives. The most famous practitioner in that category was the Cretan poet and freedman of the emperor Hadrian, Mesomedes, whose distinctive rhythms are parodied in Lucian's mock-tragic verse work entitled *Gout*. The other major strand of Imperial poetry can be categorised by its metre – the hexameter – the traditional metre of epic and didactic verse (although some epigrams were composed in hexameter too). In the former category of epic there is relatively little surviving work. We have to look much later, to the Christian world of the fifth century, to see the renewed flourishing of pagan epic, in poems like Nonnus' *Dionysiaka*, which describes the conquest of India by the god Dionysus. But there is enough Imperial-period epic attested to make it clear that there was a continuous tradition stretching from the Hellenistic to the late antique period. The most important example is Quintus of Smyrna's *Posthomerica*, which deals with events at Troy after the end of the *Iliad* – although it is important to stress that the date of the text is controversial, and some place it as late as the fifth century, roughly contemporary with Nonnus. In other cases we have to rely on tantalising snippets of information about poems which do not survive: for example Philostratus tells us that the sophist Scopelian composed a widely imitated epic entitled the *Gigantias* (or *Epic of the Giants*).

Didactic poetry survives in more bulk than epic. One important example is Dionysius of Alexandria's *Periegesis*, a geographical poem, probably published in the 130s, which surveys the known world in not much more than 1,000 lines. It is interesting here to see the geographical, knowledge-ordering obsessions of Imperial prose literature replicated in verse. That is another sign that verse should not be separated off entirely, as a literary backwater, from the dominant prose trends (although the traditions of didactic poetry, like compilatory prose, stretch back by many centuries – this is not just an interest of the Imperial period). Other examples – many of which we know about by hearsay, rather than because the texts themselves survive – include poems on medicine, astrology, birds, hunting and fishing. Particularly accomplished in this last category

is Oppian's *Halieutica*, probably published in the late 180s, which cata-
logues different types of fish and a variety of different ways of catching
them. The poem is full of epic-style similes which compare the lives of
the fish with human characters and situations and which imply parallels
between human and piscine passions and skills. Oppian's anthropomorphising approach to the fish kingdom has much in common with Aelian's
prose miscellany *On Animals*, discussed in Chapter 5, and written several
decades later. In Oppian, the battle between fisherman and fish is represented, in line with that anthropomorphising perspective, as a contest
between worthy adversaries. A similar anthropomorphising concern is
differently manifested in the continued interest in writing verse fables:
most importantly in the work of the first- or second-century poet Babrius.

Poetry was written, then, and written in some cases by individuals with
high literary reputations, but it was rarely in itself a route to literary
prestige. Why, then – and in conclusion – was prose so dominant? One
answer may lie in changing conceptions of what authorship involved or
required. In a society so heavily aware of the rich body of older literature
and culture lying behind it, the focus seems to have shifted from an
emphasis on poetic innovation – the author speaking in quasi-oracular
style with the words given to him by the inspiration of the Muses – to an
emphasis on the importance of rearranging and rephrasing the words of
others, sorting through the literature of the past and situating oneself in
relation to it, a task which is more suited to the precise and human tones
of the Greco-Roman prose tradition (although that is not to suggest that
the prestige of prose was a new thing – it dates right back to the democratic
culture of classical Athens, linked with the new importance ascribed in
that context to rhetorical persuasion). That assumption about the power
of prose to reproduce and transmit tradition seems to have been inherited
by early Christian culture, for which prose was the standard vehicle for
theological debate, and indeed for religious revelation, on the model of
the Hebrew Old Testament and early-Christian writing in the New Testament and elsewhere. Christian preference for prose may in turn have
influenced the high survival rates of Greco-Roman prose texts from the
first to third centuries, partly because so many of these Greco-Roman texts
had themselves provided important models for Christian genres (as we
saw above in Chapter 4 for the use of Greco-Roman philosophy by
Christian apologists).

That is not to suggest, however, that we should retreat to an old model
of Imperial Greek literature as degenerate and derivative. On the contrary,
the pose of author as inheritor and imitator and transformer of the heritage
of the past was both highly prestigious and entirely compatible with

enormously inventive and creative literary composition. Prose had, from its very beginnings in the culture of fifth century Greece, been associated with novelty and modernity, challenging the entrenched authority of poetic speech with a new scientific rigour, and new precision in the quest for understanding of cause and motivation (as Simon Goldhill has shown – see Further reading). Those connotations seem all the more relevant to the Greek authors of the Roman Empire, who are so saturated in the poetry of the past, and so obsessed with imitating it. By doing so in prose – for example in Aristides' writing of prose hymns to the gods (although Aristides wrote verse hymns as well) – they create a defamiliarising effect, proclaiming the newness of their own reactivation of the voices and personas of the past.

One final, and closely connected factor, is the generic flexibility of prose, in other words its capacity to incorporate many other genres within it. One of the most prominent themes of this book has been the extraordinary generic fluidity of this period's literature. By that I mean both the fluidity and ingenuity with which it cannibalises the many and varied genres of the past, and also the high degree of cross-fertilisation between different kinds of composition I have sketched out in these chapters. We have seen repeatedly that none of the chapter headings I have chosen really works: each one threatens to spill out beyond its own boundaries. Even the boundary between philosophy and oratory – which was vehemently protected by many ancient intellectuals – is often impossible to uphold in practice, perhaps not surprisingly in a system when so many young men studied both side by side. The compilatory tendencies which we find in the fields of scientific and miscellanistic writing similarly leave their mark in many other kinds of writing. Lucian's satire is itself almost by definition parasitic: it functions by taking on the form of other existing genres and subverting them, exposing their absurdity, rather than being in any sense a recognisable genre of its own. By those standards, the Greek novel, whose problematic generic identity has often been discussed in modern scholarship – there is, after all, no word for 'novel' in ancient Greek – comes, paradoxically, to look more, rather than less securely bounded than many of the other genres of Greek Imperial literature.

None of this fluidity would be possible without prose. Poetic writing in the ancient world tends to be highly marked in generic terms. There are exceptions – poetic texts which situate themselves on the boundaries between different genres. The dazzlingly inventive poems of the Hellenistic genius Callimachus are an obvious case in point, and an important reminder that generic boundary-crossing is not exclusive to the Roman world. But on the whole it is clear when one is writing epic or tragedy or iambic, not least because the metre of a poem – the very form of the text – is so often closely tied to its function. Prose too has its own genres – historiography or epideictic oratory or miscellany – but the markers of genre tend to be much less secure. Prose can switch between many different signals of genre at will. Scholarship on the ancient novel has often seen it as a genre which is marked by capacity to incorporate many different types of writing into a single text. That characterisation has some force, I suggest, not just for the novels, but also for Imperial Greek literature as a whole. One of the most wonderful things about reading these texts, at their best, is the fascination and complexity of the many-layered voices they confront us with. The fascination with speaking voice and authorial identity is one which many Imperial Greek writers share. We have seen already how Philostratus is obsessed with capturing and characterising the voices of his sophistic subjects. We have seen, too, the importance of authorial self-portrayal for authors like Dio and Lucian, who love experimenting with different masks and personas. Some of that same mingling of voices is apparent within the compilatory literature of the period, which is so interested in the challenge of bringing to life the voices of the authors of the past. The voices of Imperial Greek literature are above all prose voices, but they are not for that reason flatter or more prosaic: rather, prose is the vehicle which makes possible Imperial Greek literature's enormous freshness and hybridity and variety.

Suggestions for Further Reading

General

Important general works on the literature of this period include E. Bowie, 'Greeks and their past in the Second Sophistic', in M.I. Finley (ed.) *Studies in Ancient Society* (London 1974): 166-209 (revised version; first published in 1970); S. Swain, *Hellenism and Empire: Language, Classicism, and Power in the Greek World AD 50-250* (Oxford 1996); T. Whitmarsh, *Greek Literature and the Roman Empire: The Politics of Imitation* (Oxford 2001). Bowie discusses Imperial Greek literature's fascination with the past, and sees it as reaction to political disempowerment; Swain examines the attitudes of Greek Imperial authors to Rome; Whitmarsh challenges traditional views of the literature of this period as secondary and derivative. See also S. Goldhill (ed.) *Being Greek under Rome: Cultural Identity, the Second Sophistic and Development of Empire* (Cambridge 2001) for a challenging collection of essays; J. König, *Athletics and Literature in the Roman Empire* (Cambridge 2005) for discussion of the way in which Imperial Greek literature engages with the world around it, and specifically with the contemporary craze for athletic training and athletic competition.

Novels

All the Greek texts discussed in this chapter are available in good English translation in B.P. Reardon (ed.) *Collected Ancient Greek Novels* (Berkeley 1989; 2nd edn 2008). Longus is available in both Penguin (tr. P. Turner, 1956) and Oxford World's Classics (tr. R. McCail, 2002). Also available, in the Oxford World's Classics series, is Achilles Tatius, *Leucippe and Clitophon* (tr. T. Whitmarsh, 2003, with excellent introduction by H. Morales, whose book on Achilles Tatius – *Vision and Narrative in Achilles Tatius' Leucippe and Clitophon* (Cambridge 2004) – is also important). The most important fragments are translated at the end of the Reardon volume; for a fuller collection, see S. Stephens and J. Winkler (eds) *Ancient Greek Novels: The Fragments* (Princeton 1995). Translations of the Apocryphal Acts are available in J. Elliott (ed.) *The Apocryphal New Testament: A Collection of Apocryphal Christian Literature in an English Translation* (Oxford 1993). Good introductory works on the Greek novels include H. Hofmann, *Latin Fiction: The Latin Novel in Context* (London 1999); J.R. Morgan and R. Stoneman (eds) *Greek Fiction: The Greek Novel in Context* (London 1994); T. Whitmarsh (ed.) *The Cambridge Companion to the Greek and Roman Novel* (Cambridge 2008). Extensive discussion of the relation between ancient and modern novel traditions is available in M. Doody, *The True Story of the Novel* (New Brunswick, NJ 1996). For discussion of the relationship between the novels and the canonical Acts of the Apostles, see L. Alexander, *Acts in its Ancient Literary Context: A Classicist Looks at the Acts of the Apostles* (London 2007), chs 4 and 6.

Lucian

All Lucian's works are available in translation in the Loeb Classical Library series; in addition, translations of selected works are available in Penguin (tr. K. Sidwell, 2004: *Lucian: Chattering Courtesans and Other Sardonic Sketches*, including *Nigrinus* and *True Stories*) and Oxford World's Classics (tr. C.D.N. Costa, 2005: *Lucian: Selected Dialogues*, including *Icaromenippus, Nigrinus* and *True Stories*). At the time of writing, translations of all Lucian's works are also available online at http://www.sacred-texts.com/cla/luc/index.htm. For analysis, see C.P. Jones, *Culture and Society in Lucian* (Cambridge, MA 1986) on Lucian's relations with the society of the Roman Empire; R.B. Branham, *Unruly Eloquence: Lucian and the Comedy of Traditions* (Cambridge, MA 1989) on Lucianic humour, which I have drawn on heavily in my discussion of the *Symposium*; Whitmarsh (2001) ch. 5 (see under 'General' above), which I have drawn on heavily in my discussion of the *On Salaried Posts*; König (2005) ch. 2 (see under 'General' above) on the *Anacharsis*; I. Lada-Richards, *Silent Eloquence: Lucian and Pantomime Dancing* (London 2007) on Lucian's *On the Dance*.

Oratory

Philostratus' *Lives of the Sophists* and the orations of Dio of Prusa are available in the Loeb Classical Library series, as are some of the works of Aelius Aristides (including his *Panathenaicus*). For full translation of Aristides' works, see C.A. Behr, *The Complete Works: P. Aelius Aristides* (2 vols) (Leiden 1981-6). Favorinus' *Corinthian Oration* was erroneously handed down as *Oration* 37 in Dio's corpus of speeches, and is included as such in the Loeb Dio volumes. For Menander Rhetor, see D.A. Russell and N.G. Wilson, *Menander Rhetor* (Oxford 1981). On sophistic oratory, the best introduction is T. Whitmarsh, *The Second Sophistic* (Oxford 2005); important also is M. Gleason, *Making Men: Sophists and Self-Presentation in Ancient Rome* (Princeton 1995), who focuses in particular on the quarrel between Favorinus and Polemo; and G. Bowersock, *Greek Sophists in the Roman Empire* (Oxford 1969). On Menander Rhetor, see M. Heath, *Menander: A Rhetor in Context* (Oxford 2004). On Favorinus' *Corinthian Oration*, see J. König, 'Favorinus' *Corinthian Oration* in its Corinthian context', *Proceedings of the Cambridge Philological Society* 47 (2001): 141-71. On Dio of Prusa, see the essays in S. Swain (ed.) *Dio Chrysostom: Politics, Letters and Philosophy* (Oxford 2000); C.P. Jones, *The Roman World of Dio Chrysostom* (Cambridge, MA 1978); also, on the Kingship Orations, Whitmarsh (2001) ch. 4 (see under 'General' above), which I have drawn on heavily in my discussion of those texts in this chapter. For discussion of engagement with (and rejection of) sophistic rhetoric in early Christian writing, see B. Winter, *Philo and Paul among the Sophists* (Cambridge 1997).

Philosophy

See above under 'Sophistic oratory' for Dio of Prusa. For translation and discussion of the works of Maximus of Tyre, see M. Trapp, *Maximus of Tyre: The Philosophical Orations* (Oxford 1997). The *Meditations* of Marcus Aurelius are translated in the Oxford World's Classics series (tr. A.S.L. Farquharson, 1998); for analysis see P. Hadot, *The Inner Citadel: The Meditations of Marcus Aurelius* (Cambridge, MA 1998). Translations of Epictetus are available in the Loeb Classical Library series; and for discussion see A.A. Long, *Epictetus: A Stoic and Socratic Guide to Life* (Oxford 2002), which helpfully includes translation of a large number of sample passages. For translation and discussion of Diogenes of Oenoanda, see M.F. Smith, *The Epicurean Inscription: Diogenes of Oenoanda* (Naples 1993). The best broad introduction to the philosophy of the period is M. Trapp, *Philosophy in the Roman Empire* (Aldershot 2007). There are excellent summaries of the thinking of each of the main philosophical schools, along with further reading suggestions, in the most recent (i.e. 3rd) edition of the *Oxford Classical Dictionary*. For an introductory survey of Christian engagement with Greco-Roman philosophical ideas, see H. Rhee, *Early Christian Literature: Christ and Culture in the Second and Third Centuries* (London 2005). Clement of

Alexandria's *Exhortation* is available in the Loeb Classical Library. Translation of Justin Martyr's *Dialogue with Trypho* is available in a number of versions from the first half of the last century: e.g. see the 1948 translation by T.B. Falls in the 'Fathers of the Church' series.

Science and miscellanism

Translations of Plutarch, Aelian, Gellius and Pliny are all available in the Loeb Classical Library series. Selections from Plutarch's *Moralia* are published by Penguin as *Plutarch: Essays* (tr. R. Waterfield, 1992) and *Moral Essays: Plutarch* (tr. R. Warner, 1971). The best starting-point for Galen is *Galen: Selected Works* in the Oxford World's Classics series (tr. P. Singer, 1997). Clement of Alexandria's *Stromateis* is most easily available in vol. 2 of *The Anti-Nicene Fathers* (ed. A. Roberts, J. Donaldson and A.C. Coxe (Peabody, MA 1995 (reprinted)). For analysis, see J. König and T. Whitmarsh (eds) *Ordering Knowledge in the Roman Empire* (Cambridge 2005), including general discussion of compilatory styles of composition in Imperial Greek and Latin literature in the introduction, followed by essays on a wide range of authors. For an introduction to Plutarch, see D. Russell, *Plutarch* (London 1973). For Galen, see the introduction to the Singer translation mentioned above, and chs 15 and 16 of V. Nutton, *Ancient Medicine* (London 2004). On Achilles Tatius' use of paradoxography, see H. Morales (1995) 'The taming of the view: natural curiosities in *Leukippe and Kleitophon*', *Groningen Colloquia on the Novel* 6: 39-50.

Geography/history

The works of all the authors discussed in this chapter are available in the Loeb Classical Library. In addition, for Arrian, see the Penguin translation (by A. de Selincourt, 1971) entitled *Arrian: The Campaigns of Alexander*; and for Pausanias, the Penguin translation by Peter Levi (1971, 2 vols). For discussion of the interrelation between geography and history, and of Strabo, see K. Clarke, *Between Geography and History: Hellenistic Constructions of the Roman World* (Oxford 1999); on Strabo, see also D. Dueck, *Strabo: A Greek Man of Letters in Augustan Rome* (London 2000). For Pausanias, see M. Pretzler, *Pausanias: Travel Writing in Roman Greece* (London 2007); W. Hutton, *Describing Greece: Landscape and Literature in the Periegesis of Pausanias* (Cambridge 2005); and ch. 4 of König (2005) (see under 'General' above) on Pausanias' visit to Olympia. For overview discussion of the Greek historians of the Imperial period, see (in this series) T. Duff, *The Greek and Roman Historians* (London 2003), ch. 11.

Biography

All the authors discussed in this chapter are available in the Loeb Classical Library series. In addition there are several collections of Plutarch's *Lives* published by Penguin: *Makers of Rome* (tr. I. Scott-Kilvert, 1965); *The Age of Alexander* (tr. I. Scott-Kilvert, 1973); *The Rise and Fall of Athens* (tr. I. Scott-Kilvert, 1960); *Fall of the Roman Republic* (tr. R. Warner, 1972). For Lucian, the *Demonax, Alexander* and *Peregrinus* are all available in Costa's Oxford World's Classics translation; the *Demonax* is also available in Sidwell's Penguin translation (see under 'Lucian' above). For general discussion of Greek biography, see A. Momigliano, *The Development of Greek Biography* (Cambridge, MA 1993), though focusing mainly on the pre-Roman period; and for good recent essays on the biographical writing of the Imperial period, see M. Edwards and S. Swain, *Portraits: Biographical Representation in the Greek and Latin Literature of the Roman Empire* (Oxford 1997) and B. McGing and J. Mossman (eds) *The Limits of Ancient Biography* (Swansea 2006). On Plutarch, see T. Duff, *Plutarch's Lives: Exploring Virtue and Vice* (Oxford 1999), especially ch. 3 on Plutarch's interest in the balance between reason and passion in the human soul, which I have drawn on heavily in the relevant section of this chapter; C. Pelling, *Plutarch and History: Eighteen Studies* (London 2002); and see also Russell (1973) (under 'Science and miscellanism' above). On Philostratus, see Whitmarsh (2005) (see under 'Oratory' above). On Lucian, see Jones (1986) (see under 'Lucian' above) for the historical background to these two works; Branham (1989) (see under 'Lucian' above) on the *Alexander*; and on the *Peregrinus*, J. König, 'The Cynic and Christian Lives of Lucian's *Peregrinus*' in McGing and Mossman (eds) (above): 227-54.

Poetry

The works of Oppian and Quintus of Smyrna are available in the Loeb Classical Library series, as are the epigrams of the Palatine Anthology, many of which date from the first to third centuries CE (in the Loeb volumes entitled *Greek Anthology*; see esp. Book 11 for Lucillius). For analysis, see E. Bowie, 'Greek poetry in the Antonine age', in D. Russell (ed.) *Antonine Literature* (Oxford 1990): 53-90; E. Bowie, 'Greek sophists and Greek poetry in the Second Sophistic', in *Aufstieg und Nieder-*

gang der Römischen Welt 2.33.1 (1989): 209-58; G. Nisbet, *Greek Epigram in the Roman Empire: Martial's Forgotten Rivals* (Oxford 2003). For the importance of prose in this period, see the final chapter of S. Goldhill, *The Invention of Prose* (Oxford 2002) (also earlier chapters of that book on the role of prose in classical Athenian culture).

Questions for Further Study and Discussion

Novels

- What role does the character of Kalasiris play in Heliodorus' *Ethiopian Tale*? (further discussion in J. Winkler, 'The mendacity of Kalasiris and the narrative strategy of Heliodoros' *Aithiopika*', *Yale Classical Studies* 27 (1982) 93-158, reprinted in S. Swain (ed.) *Oxford Readings in the Greek Novel* (Oxford 1999)).
- Discuss the representation of violence in Longus' *Daphnis and Chloe* (further discussion in J. Winkler, *Constraints of Desire: The Anthropology of Sex and Gender in Ancient Greece* (London 1990) ch. 4).
- Discuss the representation of vision in Achilles Tatius' *Leukippe and Kleitophon* (further discussion in H. Morales, *Vision and Narrative in Achilles Tatius'* Leucippe and Clitophon (Cambridge 2004)).

Lucian

- How does Lucian's *True Stories* use its fantastic tales of strange lands to reflect on Greek identity and Greek tradition?
- How does Lucian represent the city of Rome and the activities of Greek intellectuals there in his *Nigrinus*?

Sophistic oratory

- How does Dio represent himself in the first half of *Oration* 36, his account of his journey to the city of Borysthenes? How does that work represent Greek culture?
- Discuss the portrayal of Favorinus and Aelius Aristides and Dio in Philostratus' *Lives of the Sophists*. How do these sections compare with his portrayals of the other sophists?

Philosophy

- Read as much as possible of the work of Epictetus and Marcus Aurelius. What similarities and differences do you see between them? In what ways does the form of their writing contribute to their philosophical message?

- Read through Dio of Prusa *Orations* 8 and 9. In what ways does Dio use the Cynic philosopher Diogenes as a model for his own persona? Do you see any serious philosophical purpose in these two texts? In what ways do they overlap with the philosophical principles he advocates elsewhere in his work?

Science and miscellanism

- Work through the Galen texts in Singer's translation (Oxford World's Classics). How do these texts represent the intellectual traditions and professional relationships Galen was involved in? How does Galen represent himself in these texts?
- Work through the first book of Plutarch's *Sympotic Questions*. What do Plutarch, and the speakers he describes, achieve by quoting so heavily from earlier authors? To what degree and in what ways is his work meant to be a guide for behaviour at a symposium?

Geography/history

- Read as much as possible of Arrian's *Campaigns of Alexander*. How do you account for Arrian's fascination with geography in this work and elsewhere? How does Arrian's use of geographical detail contribute to his characterisation of Alexander and his conquests?
- Read as much of Pausanias' work as possible. What similarities and differences do you see in relation to modern guide books? How do you explain the differences? What similarities and differences do you see between Pausanias and other authors from this period in their representation of the Greek past?

Biography

- Read through any one pair of Plutarch's biographies. How does the pair you have chosen represent (a) education and (b) passion? To what extent does Plutarch appear to be interested in change or development of character over time? How do your chosen biographies function as a pair? What interrelations do you see between them? (N.B. the Penguin volumes of Plutarch translations noted under 'Further reading' break up the pairs of lives: consult the Loeb Classical Library for the original pairings).
- Read through Lucian's *Alexander*. In what ways is this text similar to and different from modern biographical writing, and how do you account for the differences? How does the work represent the relations between Alexander and his various audiences? And how does that

representation of audience relate to similar themes in other works of Lucian you have looked at?

General

- How far and in what ways does the Greek literature of this period engage with the realities of Roman rule? Do you see any sign of the answer to that question changing over time?
- Discuss the ways in which Imperial Greek literature rewrites key texts of earlier Greek literature (e.g. see Dio of Prusa, *Oration* 11 for an example of the rewriting of Homer's *Iliad*; Lucian's *True Stories* or Heliodorus' *Ethiopian Tale* for rewriting of Homer's *Odyssey*; Lucian's *Symposium* for rewriting of Plato's *Symposium*). Homer and Plato are the two most often quoted texts in the Greek literature of this period. How should we account for that prominence? What similarities and differences do you see in the way they are treated?

Timeline

The table below includes all first- to third-century CE authors discussed at any length in this volume. Authors are listed very roughly in chronological order, but the ordering is necessarily highly approximate, partly because many of these writers had careers stretching over so many decades, and partly because it is impossible to be clear about the dates of many. Where an author's dates of birth and death are known or approximately known they are included; in other cases, where our knowledge of those dates is imprecise, the abbreviation fl. (standing for Latin *floruit*, 'flourished') has sometimes been used to indicate very roughly the date of the high-point of an author's career. These datings are based, with some adjustments, on those in the most recent (i.e. third) edition of the *Oxford Classical Dictionary*. Latin authors mentioned in the text are included in italics. Christian authors are asterisked.

	Authors	**Emperors**

1st cent. BCE	Strabo (64-after 21 CE)
	 Dionysius of Halicarnassus
	   (fl. late 1st cent. BCE)
	 Horace (65-8)
		Augustus
		   (31 BCE-14 CE)

1st cent. CE	Lucillius (fl. 60)
	 Heron of Alexandria (fl. 62)
	 Musonius (c. 30-c. 100)
	 Josephus (37/8-after 93)
	 Dio of Prusa (40s?-after 110)
	 Plutarch (before 50-120
	   approx.)
	 Epictetus (mid-first to early
	   second century)
	 Chariton?
	 Martial (c. 40-c. 100)
	 Petronius (fl. 60?)
	 Pliny the Elder (23/4-79)
	 Pliny the Younger (61-112
	   approx.)
		Tiberius (14-37)
		 Caligula (37-41)
		 Claudius (41-54)
		 Nero (54-68)
		 Galba (68-69)
		 Otho (69)
		 Vitellius (69)
		 Vespasian (69-79)
		 Titus (79-81)
		 Domitian (81-96)
		 Nerva (96-98)

	Authors	Emperors
2nd cent. CE	Favorinus (c. 85-c. 155) Arrian (86-160) Mesomedes (fl. 144) Aelius Aristides (117-after 181) Marcus Aurelius (121-80) Pausanias (fl. 150?) Lucian (b. c. 120?) Galen (129-early 3rd cent.) Oppian (fl. late 2nd cent.?) Maximus of Tyre? Longus? Achilles Tatius? Dionysius of Alexandria ('the Periegete')? Diogenes of Oenoanda? Babrius? Xenophon of Ephesus? *Juvenal* (fl. early 2nd cent.) *Tacitus* (c. 56-after 118) *Suetonius* (70-130 approx.?) *Apuleius* (b. c. 125?) *Aulus Gellius* (b. c. 125?) *Apocryphal Acts of the Apostles (some 3rd cent. and later) *Justin (c. 100-c. 165) *Tatian (fl. 170?) *Clement of Alexandria (c. 150-c. 215)	Trajan (98-117) Hadrian (117-138) Antoninus Pius (138-161) Marcus Aurelius (161-180) Lucius Verus (161-169) Commodus (180-192) Septimius Severus (193-211)

	Authors	Emperors
3rd cent. CE	Aelian (165/70-230/5) Herodian (fl. early 3rd cent.) Cassius Dio (164 approx.-after 229) Philostratus (late 2nd cent.-245 approx.) Plotinus (205-269/70) Porphyry (c. 234-c. 305) Heliodorus? Diogenes Laertius? Quintus of Smyrna? Athenaeus? Menander Rhetor? *Tertullian* (c. 160-c. 240)	Caracalla (211-217) Macrinus (217-218) Elagabalus (218-222) Alexander Severus (222-235) The period of the third-century crisis (from 235 to 284) saw more than twenty individuals proclaimed emperor at different times – a full list is not provided here. From 293, the empire was ruled by the Tetrarchy, with power divided between four individuals (two senior and two junior emperors). The Tetrarchy was instituted by the emperor Diocletian, who was emperor from 284 to his abdication in 305.
4th cent. CE	*Eusebius (260-339)	Constantine (306-337)

Index

Achilles Tatius 14, 15-16, 19-20, 21, 76
Acts of the Apostles 97
Aelian 73-4, 75, 76, 102
Aelius Aristides 46-8, 103
  On Athens 47-8, 61
  Sacred Tales 50-1
Aeschines 42
Alexander the Great 49-50, 77, 78, 81
Alexandria 8, 66
Antonius Diogenes 23
Apocryphal Acts of the Apostles 23-4, 64
Apollodorus of Pergamon 42
Appian 77, 78, 80
Apuleius 22
Aristophanes 30, 31, 42
Aristotle 45, 55, 56, 66, 86
Arrian 59, 77, 78, 80
Athenaeus 31, 71
Athens 8, 28, 41, 43, 47-8, 56, 81-5, 102
athletics 28-9, 99, 100
Attic Greek 8, 36
Augustine 61
Augustus 7, 42, 80, 86, 87, 88, 95
Aulus Gellius 70, 74-5
autobiography 26, 68

Babrius 101
biography 26, 58, 86-98

Callimachus 103
Cassius Dio 77-8, 80
Chaironeia 71
Chariton 13, 14-15, 21

Christian literature 8, 24-5, 45, 56, 61, 63-5, 72-3, 78, 92-3, 97, 102
Christianity (see also Christian literature) 94-5
Chrysippus 56
Cicero 42, 61, 88
Clement of Alexandria 64, 72-3
comedy 17, 29, 69
Constantine 78, 93
Corinth 48

democracy 43, 53
Demosthenes 37, 42, 91
dialogue 17, 26, 58, 64
Dio of Prusa (Dio Chrysostom) 23, 49-53, 54-5, 58, 60, 97, 104
  Euboian Oration 52-3, 54
Diogenes Laertius 86, 89-90
Diogenes of Oenoanda 61-3, 65
Dionysius of Alexandria ('the Periegete') 101
Dionysius of Halicarnassus 42, 77
Domitian 51

education 9, 36, 41, 45, 56-7, 58-9, 75, 88
Eleusis 83
elite identity 14, 19-21
encyclopaedism 37, 67, 75, 79
epic 17, 101, 103
Epictetus 59-60, 61, 65, 77
Epicurus 56, 68, 89
epigram 99-101
Eratosthenes 81
ethics 56-7
ethnography 13-14, 21-2, 24-5, 78

Eusebius 78, 93

Favorinus 48-9, 50, 51, 58, 66, 90,
    91, 97

Galen 56, 68-70, 72, 79
genre 9, 17-18, 103-4
geography 68, 77-85, 101
gods 29, 31, 37-8, 50-1, 64, 95-7
Gorgias 42
Greek identity 13-14, 21-2, 26-7, 28,
    38-9, 46, 48-9

Hadrian 75, 84, 101
Heliodorus 9, 11-12, 14, 18-22
Heraclitus 89
Herakles 94
Herodes Atticus 43-4, 45, 58, 66,
    74-5, 83, 84-5, 90, 93, 99
Herodian 77
Herodotus 14, 26, 78, 84
heroes, Homeric 41, 90
Heron of Alexandria 68
Hippocrates 68, 69
Historia Augusta 86-7
historiography 17, 26, 68, 77-85
Homer 38, 41, 59, 79-80
    Iliad 32, 90, 101
    Odyssey 17, 18, 20-1, 22, 23,
        39-40, 100
honour 42, 44, 58, 62
Horace 27

Iamblichos 23
intellectual genealogy 44, 89
Isocrates 47

Jewish literature 63-4, 78, 102
Josephus 78
Julius Caesar 42, 87
Justin 64-5
Juvenal 27

Libanius 45

Lollianos 23
Longus 14-15, 17, 19, 52
Lucian 9, 26-40, 49, 50, 55, 56, 60,
    63, 101, 103, 104
    Alexander 36, 93-4
    Anacharsis 28-9
    Demonax 36, 93-4
    Dialogues of the Gods 37
    Icaromenippus 29-31, 32-3, 37, 38
    On the Dance 36
    On Salaried Posts 28, 34-6, 71
    Peregrinus 36, 93-5
    Symposium 31-3, 37, 71
    True Stories 23-4, 31, 38-40
Lucillius 99-100
Lucretius 61
lyric poetry 17, 101

Marcus Aurelius 57, 59, 60-1, 62, 64,
    70, 90
Mark Antony 7, 88-9
Martial 100
Maximus of Tyre 58-9, 79
Menander Rhetor 44-6, 47, 49
Menippean satire 27
Mesomedes 101
miscellanism 37, 58, 66, 67, 70-5, 79,
    103
Musonius 61

Nero 85
novels, ancient 9, 11-25, 26, 40, 52,
    68, 103
novels, modern 11-12

Oenoanda 62
Olympia 83, 95
Oppian 102

paradoxography 75
pastoral 15, 17, 52-3
Paul 63
Pausanias 19, 79, 81-5
Petronius 22, 27

philosophy, philosophers 17, 21, 26, 29-36, 40, 41, 50, 51-2, 54-65, 66, 68-72, 79, 80, 93-8, 103
  Aristotelians, Peripatetics 33, 55, 58, 64
  Cynics 27, 33, 54, 55, 94
  Epicureans 33, 55, 56, 58, 61-3, 68, 89
  Neoplatonists 56
  Platonists, Academics 33, 55, 56, 58, 64, 72
  Pythagoreans 55, 92
  Sceptics 55
  Stoics 33, 55, 56, 58, 59-60, 64, 73, 79
Philostratus
  Heroicus 52
  Life of Apollonius 92
  Lives of the Sophists 8, 41, 42-4, 45, 50, 51, 56, 74, 86, 90-2, 96, 101, 104
Phlegon 75
Photius 22
Plato 17, 26, 42, 55, 56, 57, 58, 59, 68, 69
  Symposium 31, 35, 71
Pliny the Elder 67, 75
Pliny the Younger 51
Plotinus 56
Plutarch 9, 31, 58, 70-2, 73, 76, 77, 80
  Lives 72, 87-9, 90, 98
  Sympotic Questions 70-2
poetry 68, 99-102
Polemo 43-4, 45, 66, 90, 91-2
Polybius 77, 78
Porphyry 56
prose 99, 101-4
Protagoras 42
Prusa 51
Ptolemy 79
Pythagoras 89

Quintilian 27
Quintus of Smyrna 101

rhetoric 13, 28, 36-7, 41-53, 55, 58-9, 63, 102, 103
rhetors 43
Rome, Romans 7-8, 28, 34-6, 41, 43, 61, 74-5, 77-8, 80-1, 83-5, 86-7, 91, 97-8

Samosata 26
Sappho 17
satire, ancient 26-40
satire, modern 23, 26, 27, 34
science 41, 57, 66, 68-90, 103
'Second Sophistic' 8
Socrates 30, 31, 35, 54, 59, 94
sophists 8, 23, 26, 37, 40, 41-53, 58, 90-2
Strabo 79-81, 82, 84, 85
Suetonius 61, 86, 87
symposium 31-6, 70-2, 80

Tacitus 61
Tatian 64
Tertullian 64
Theodoros of Gadara 42
Thucydides 17
Tiberius 42
tragedy 17, 29, 103
Trajan 49, 51

Varro 27
vision 20, 32-3, 34-5, 76

women in the Greek novels 16-17, 18-21, 76

Xenophon 59, 71 77
Xenophon of Ephesus 14, 86

Zeno 56

Lightning Source UK Ltd.
Milton Keynes UK
UKHW020249090921
390279UK00008B/193